Praise for *Customer-Driven Disruption*

"Suman Sarkar redirects the focus back to what made your business a business: its customers. With many case studies and concise takeaways, this book is a handy guide to shaking up your innovation strategy."
—**Crystal Kadakia, author of** *The Millennial Myth*

"Suman Sarkar is a strategist after my own heart—like me, he believes that real change and innovation come from customers' actual needs and wants, not from researchers in lab coats. Customers *will* tell you how to make your business thrive and win the future—if you learn how to listen. This book explains how to open your ears."
—**Jeanne Bliss, President, CustomerBliss, and author of** *Chief Customer Officer 2.0*

"Sarkar puts forth new, actionable definitions of customer focus, personalization, and quality along with a road map that your team can use to think creatively and be more willing to take intelligent risks."
—**John A. Goodman, Vice Chairman, Customer Care Measurement & Consulting**

"This is an excellent, thought-provoking book that offers clear strategies enabling you to understand buying patterns and generational expectations. *Customer-Driven Disruption* will inspire you to effectively plan for and stay ahead of your competition by focusing on your customers and what they want."
—**Renee Evenson, author of nine books including** *Powerful Phrases for Effective Customer Service* **and** *Powerful Phrases for Dealing with Difficult People*

"In *Customer-Driven Disruption*, Sarkar shows that technology isn't the real driver of disruption, and he unveils many more surprises that will challenge your assumptions and prepare you and your organization to stay ahead."
—**Steve Curtin, author of** *Delight Your Customers*

CUSTOMER-DRIVEN
DISRUPTION

CUSTOMER-DRIVEN
DISRUPTION

FIVE STRATEGIES TO STAY AHEAD OF THE CURVE

SUMAN SARKAR

AUTHOR OF *THE SUPPLY CHAIN REVOLUTION*

BK°

Berrett–Koehler Publishers, Inc.
www.bkconnection.com

Berrett-Koehler Publishers, Inc.
1333 Broadway, Suite 1000
Oakland, CA 94612-1921
Tel: (510) 817-2277
Fax: (510) 817-2278
www.bkconnection.com

ORDERING INFORMATION
Quantity sales. Special discounts are available on quantity purchases by corporations, associations, and others. For details, contact the "Special Sales Department" at the Berrett-Koehler address above.

Individual sales. Berrett-Koehler publications are available through most bookstores. They can also be ordered directly from Berrett-Koehler: Tel: (800) 929-2929; Fax: (802) 864-7626; www.bkconnection.com.

Orders for college textbook / course adoption use. Please contact Berrett-Koehler: Tel: (800) 929-2929; Fax: (802) 864-7626.

Distributed to the U.S. trade and internationally by Penguin Random House Publisher Services.

Berrett-Koehler and the BK logo are registered trademarks of Berrett-Koehler Publishers, Inc.

Printed in Canada

Berrett-Koehler books are printed on long-lasting acid-free paper. When it is available, we choose paper that has been manufactured by environmentally responsible processes. These may include using trees grown in sustainable forests, incorporating recycled paper, minimizing chlorine in bleaching, or recycling the energy produced at the paper mill.

Library of Congress Cataloging-in-Publication Data

Names: Sarkar, Suman, author.
Title: Customer-driven disruption : five strategies to stay ahead of the curve / Suman Sarkar.
Description: Oakland, CA : Berrett-Koehler Publishers, Inc., [2019]
Identifiers: LCCN 2019014366 | ISBN 9781523099757 (print hardcover)
Subjects: LCSH: Customer relations. | Strategic planning.
Classification: LCC HF5415.5 .S2735 2019 | DDC 658.8/12--dc23
LC record available at https://lccn.loc.gov/2019014366

First Edition
25 24 23 22 21 20 19   10 9 8 7 6 5 4 3 2 1

Interior design and production: Seventeenth Street Studios
Cover design: The BookDesigners
Copyedit: Todd Manza
Index: Richard Evans

This book is dedicated to the memory
of my mother, Dipti Sarkar,
and my father, Ranjan Sarkar,
for their love, encouragement, and support.

CONTENTS

PREFACE

I'M A BUSINESS CONSULTANT, and my neighbor is the CFO of a Fortune 100 company; we talk about our work a lot. We once spent an entire barbecue talking about supply chains. So of course I told him about this book, and I was taken aback when he said, "Why are you writing about customers? Every business leader knows customers are important. It's a cliché. You're talking motherhood and apple pie."

"If you put it like that, yes. But knowing and doing are two different things."

This book is about the doing. Even executives who claim that customers are important don't always know what their customers' needs are or how to deliver them. Some know but are afraid to try. And some won't even try. Over the years, I've consulted with leaders at more than forty Fortune 500 companies, and meetings like the following are frustratingly common.

The CEO of a leading global delivery services company (let's call them Big D) knew that his retail customers wanted their local stores to provide home delivery; demand for that is increasing. But home delivery often costs more than the products! So Big D had another plan: convince people to pick up packages themselves until Big D had developed a drone or bot delivery system. Spending money on technology was fine with Big D's board, but the CEO knew that getting the drones to work would take so long that a start-up or Amazon would come up with a better solution first. So Big D's CEO was open to ideas, and after a conversation with someone on my team—Fred, an ex-employee of Big D, whom he respected and trusted—he told one of his executives to meet with us.

Fred and I were excited about our idea when we went in to make our pitch to Barry, the head of innovation. We'd sent him the presentation beforehand, so after the niceties were over, I said, "Hey, Barry, how do you want to do this? We've shared the presentation with you already. Do you have questions, or do you want us to start from the beginning?"

"I've read it, but start at the beginning."

So we showed him how Big D could provide same-day local delivery at half their current costs, using rented trucks and reusable packaging (another customer complaint was that people were fed up with the cardboard boxes). Barry let us go through it, but he was obviously bored. His comment was "We're Big D. We have certain standards. You're telling us to do this with chewing gum and toothpicks!"

I wanted to say "Does your customer care? When I'm getting a pizza, I don't care if it comes on a tricycle as long as I get a hot pie!" But I didn't say that; there was no point in antagonizing him. It was clear to me that he was only there because his boss's boss had told him to see us, and, like many people in the middle layer at large corporations, he would rather kill an idea than try anything that risked his position in the organization—especially anything new.

Conversations like this are incredibly frustrating to me. The book was born out of that frustration, coupled with the knowledge that companies whose leaders focus on short-term investor returns, ignore customer needs, and kill new ideas will fail. The book is a plea for change and a guide to making it. Leaders with the courage to do things differently will disrupt their industries and topple the companies whose leaders can't or won't. I hope the book inspires you to become a disrupter and shows you how to address customer needs in new, innovative ways.

Introduction
DISRUPTION MYTH

DISRUPTION—THE BRUTAL ROILING OF markets, caused by customers' ever-changing needs—drives business failure and success. Most people think that technology drives disruption, but technology merely enables disruption; changing customer needs causes it. Some companies try to recover with more innovation, more advertising, rebranding, acquisitions—and discover that these strategies do not work. Others survive disruption and even harness it to their advantage. What drives this difference? The latter group of companies keeps their focus on their customers. They understand, anticipate, and gratify their customers' needs—and thereby not only survive disruption but also thrive on it.

Consider Patanjali, a new company competing with established consumer goods companies in India. For years, Indian customers had been telling multinationals such as Hindustan Unilever, Procter & Gamble (P&G), Nestlé, and Colgate that their products were feeling harsh and not quite right on their bodies. So multinationals added moisturizers and other goodies to hide the side effects of harsher ingredients. None of the multinationals listened to Indian customers' real needs, but an Indian company, Patanjali, did. Patanjali created products from herbs and plant chemicals that are good for people's health and the environment. The products are based on Ayurveda, a traditional Indian medicinal practice. The company became a runaway success that stopped the growth of Hindustan Unilever (HUL), the Indian subsidiary of Unilever, and grabbed its market (see figure 1). By 2019, thirteen years after it started, Patanjali expects its revenue to beat HUL's—even

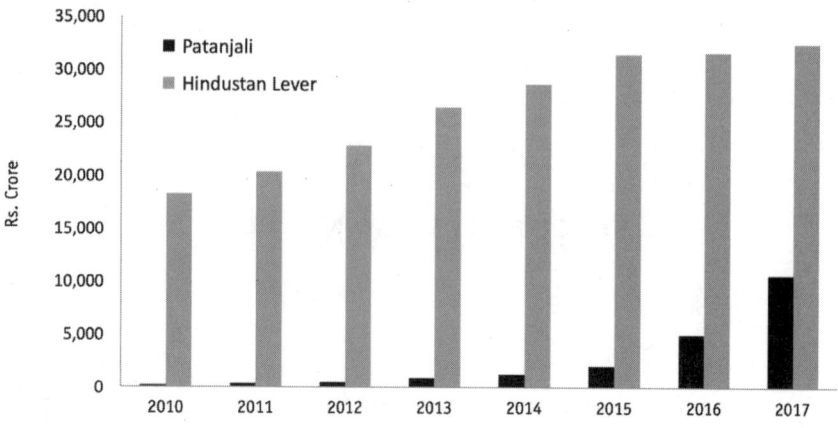

FIGURE 1 Revenue trend for Patanjali and Hindustan Unilever (a Unilever subsidiary in India). At the time of this publication, Indian Rs. 1 crore was equivalent to $150,000. Patanjali's revenue in 2017 is estimated to be $1.5 billion; Hindustan Lever's is $5 billion. Sources: "Patanjali Ayurved," Wikipedia, accessed February 18, 2019; Hindustan Unilever Limited, "Annual Report—Archives," https://goo.gl/L3RXvF.

though Unilever has dominated the Indian consumer goods market for more than eighty years.[1]

Patanjali's founders listen to their customers. They not only make products from natural ingredients but also keep them affordable by working directly with farmers rather than distributors. They keep marketing costs low by relying more on word of mouth than on advertising. In a 2017 speech, Patanjali's CEO succinctly explained the company's strategy: benefit the customers and suppliers, and the company will benefit. But you have to start with the customer. He went on to say that the organization "did not make ads with glamorous men and women but rather focused on making products that were effective. Taking a swipe at [HUL's] Close-up toothpaste, he said that his toothpaste Dant-Kanti did not make people fall in love. 'That's not the role of a toothpaste. We only make a toothpaste that cleans your teeth effectively.'"[2] Patanjali delivers on Indian customers' needs.

HUL, on the other hand, did what most failing companies do: it interpreted customer feedback within the context of its existing products instead of as a stimulus to think outside the box and change. Sanjiv

Mehta, chairman and CEO of HUL, even admitted this. He said that the company made its plans based on what they wanted their portfolio to look like, then "put disproportionate money behind innovation and building the categories of the future." But doubling down on their existing strategies by improving current products, raising prices every year, and spending more money on advertising didn't work. Now, to regain market share, HUL is copying Patanjali's use of herbs and plant chemicals. Other multinationals, such as Colgate-Palmolive, are also launching natural oral care products. But Patanjali remains the most popular with Indians because their products are great, affordable, and based on traditional Indian medicine.[3]

Stories like Patanjali's play out all over the world today. Big companies are failing, creating economic uncertainty and job insecurity, because they aren't focusing on customers. This is as true for business-to-consumer companies as it is for business-to-business companies. Fundamental shifts and changes catch up with *all* businesses and disrupt them, no matter how far they may be removed from their customers or how far downstream in the supply chain they may be. Change happens fast. If it catches your company off guard, your company will suffer—and the longer its impact has been delayed or ignored, the greater the damage will be.

But if you understand your customers and keep up with their ever-changing needs, you will be prepared for disruption and will succeed despite it. When your competitors fail because they haven't dealt with disruption, you may even grow. This book shows you how to develop the strategies to deliver services, personalization, speed, quality, and reinvention to satisfy your changing customers and their changing needs.

NEW STRATEGIES FOR DISRUPTION

Only sixty companies on the Fortune 500 list for 1955 remained on the list in 2017. That's just 12%. In addition, a Washington University study estimates that 40% of today's Fortune 500 companies won't exist in ten years.[4] They will fail because they focus on delivering short-term shareholder returns at the expense of everything else. And the more they focus on investors, the more they disconnect from what's most important to their growth and survival—their customers.

When disruption hits, these companies typically respond by disconnecting even more from their customers. They try strategies that don't work, like incremental innovation, acquisitions, rebranding or new marketing, global expansion, and even lobbying. What they ought to be doing is connecting more closely with their customers, with strategies like the following.

Customer-Focus Strategy 1: Win with Current Customers before Chasing after New Ones

Current customers are a more reliable source of revenue than new customers, but when sales drop, most companies go after new customers. In 2005, Amazon did something different with its customer base: it divided its customers into frequent and infrequent buyers. It then started what became its hugely successful Prime program, which encourages high-volume customers to buy even more.

Any company, in any industry, can increase revenue profitably by tailoring service levels to customer segments. This book teaches you how to identify customers by segments, identify the services valued by segment, create a range of services based on different customer needs, and price the new service so customers will be willing to pay for the increased service.

Customer-Focus Strategy 2: Personalization Is Not a Luxury

Personalization is replacing consumerism. The new generation of shoppers, millennials and Generation Z, love personalized service and dislike waste. You may think personalization is too expensive, but you can make it affordable. Too many companies charge too much for "specializations" or, worse, try to make money from premium services. But affordable personalization options for the many will generate far more revenues for a company than expensive select services for the few.

Using examples from companies like J. Hilburn and MTailor, which are experimenting with tailoring apparel, this book describes the challenges of personalization—such as cost and complexity—and then discusses how to change operations to produce smaller quantities cost-effectively.

To make personalization affordable, companies have to focus on flexibility throughout their operations, which is a complete change from the Industrial Revolution–era thinking of "Bigger is better." Companies can do this by rethinking customer offerings, creating flexible operations, and reducing waste. Whoever masters the art of producing affordable, personalized products will enjoy a significant competitive advantage in the future.

Customer-Focus Strategy 3: Customers Won't Wait

Customer preferences are changing, and if your company doesn't keep up, it will perish. While some apparel retailers are closing their doors, others are getting new catwalk trends into stores quickly and at affordable prices. To do this, they speed up both the design and the supply chain. They rarely do sales promotions or discount their products. Fast fashion is the fastest growing and most profitable part of the retail industry. For example, Zara started in 1988 and now has 2,200 stores in ninety-three countries, with annual revenue of $17.2 billion in 2017, and it is still increasing its market share.

Companies in all industries can learn to respond faster and succeed in the same way. That is, they can quickly develop products or solutions that address customers' changing needs, speed up the supply chain, reduce sales promotion, and produce what their customers really want to buy.

Customer-Focus Strategy 4: Good Enough Is No Longer Good Enough

Now that the public judges products based on reviews and peer recommendations, companies have to develop higher standards. Retailers such as Aldi and Lidl took over the grocery market in Europe with their focus on quality. Their products beat branded ones in head-to-head tests and independent quality reviews in Germany, and then all over Europe. They customized their product selection based on local taste. Yet, despite their higher quality, their products cost less than their competitors'.

To win with quality, you must offer a level of performance that your customers can't resist and your competition can't beat. Then you must improve on it continuously. What's stopping you from delivering that quality standard? Try doing a series of experiments—both in-house and with suppliers—to identify what's holding you back. Then optimize your operation for quality and not for throughput (volume of output). In many cases, this may mean you will have to challenge long-held misperceptions within the company or industry.

Customer-Focus Strategy 5: Disregard Strategies 1 through 4

Even adopting all the new strategies discussed so far isn't enough to keep you competitive. You must continuously revisit, revise, and have the courage to start over completely when the market calls for that.

Consider the transformation of Haier, a Chinese manufacturer of home appliances and consumer electronics. It has reinvented itself four times as customer requirements changed in China and globally. In the 1980s, they improved product quality by partnering with global companies. In the 1990s, they focused on innovation driven by customers. The Haier team looked for unique applications of their technologies, such as creating a vegetable washing machine to clean potatoes. As their competitors in China started achieving service responsiveness, Haier reorganized to keep up with changing customer needs without getting bogged down by growing in-house bureaucracy. They introduced customer-facing teams, each focused on, organized around, and expert at serving a specific market segment or big customer.

Now Haier is becoming an internet company, collaborating not only with customers but also with innovators—including competitors.

Haier began modestly in rural China and is now a leading global provider of household appliances.

If you keep changing to keep delighting customers, you will succeed. It requires keeping a sharp eye on your customers' changing needs and then figuring out how to meet those needs by thinking outside the box, engaging end users, and collaborating with experts and suppliers. Then you need to empower your teams and encourage attention to detail to implement your ideas.

FOCUS

As Samuel Johnson said, "When a man knows he is to be hanged in a fortnight, it concentrates his mind wonderfully." Disruption can be a death sentence to a business, but it doesn't have to be. You can use the threat to focus on what's important—your customers. If you use disruption to concentrate on meeting customers' needs effectively, your business can make an almost miraculous recovery.

Triumphing over disruption requires discarding old strategies and embracing new ones. It means retooling your organization's entire approach—not just products, services, and operations. You also need to change your incentives, organization, culture, and the way you recruit, train, and retain employees. Even those who already know what they need to do rarely know how to do it or where to start. This book provides a blueprint.

1

CUSTOMERS DRIVE DISRUPTION

FILENE'S BASEMENT WAS A Boston institution—tourists even came to watch customers digging through the messy bins of designer clothes. Famous for its markdowns that increased by 25% each week, Filene's Basement was the first discount retailer in the country to focus on high-end clothes. At its Running of the Brides events, excited women searched for bargain-priced wedding gowns. But most of the customers were boomers and Generation Xers and, by 2011, the famous bargain basement closed forever, like many other department stores around the country. Though people blame Amazon and online retailing for the demise of these once popular stores, the real reason is that customers' needs are changing and department stores don't meet them anymore.

It's partly that baby boomers are spending less, both because they are shrinking as a generation and because they are downsizing. So millennials are outstripping them in total spending. The two generations' needs are very different. Consumerism and buying frenzy driven by sales are foreign concepts to millennials. Name brands don't impress them the way they impress boomers and Gen Xers—millennials value service, personalization, and speed.

Retailers that are slow to bring new designs to market, can't help with style questions, and lack tailors to fit clothes—or charge extra for styling and tailoring—will never be popular with millennials. This generation, while large, doesn't have much disposable income. Millennials would rather shop at stores that charge less and address their needs better than department stores do—so they choose upstart companies. And customer needs in all industries are changing just as much—look at how Uber and Lyft disrupted the taxi and black car companies worldwide.

Every industry is at risk of disruption due to changing customer needs, and most business leaders are ill-prepared for the challenge. They don't focus on customer needs. Instead, they focus on technology, regulations, or investors. But even companies that try to focus on customers find millennials and Gen Z challenging. They are still structured around selling only to boomers and Gen X, who will pay for products, for bells and whistles, and are often swayed by advertising. But millennials would rather pay for experiences than products and features.

This 180-degree change in customer needs requires an entirely different approach on the part of companies. We can look, for example, at the automotive industry, which is still trying to sell customers new cars every year, based on new features. But as car sharing replaces car ownership, that's not going to work, no matter what upgrades new models have. Do passengers care if an Uber car is self-driving? All they want is a comfortable, safe ride in a clean car with a pleasant driver. But the car companies keep pushing self-driving vehicles. And across industries, it's the same: companies push products and services that don't match customer needs.

There are exceptions. Some companies are successfully differentiating among the generations and are addressing millennials' need for personalization. Zozotown, an undisputed leader in Japanese online fashion, introduced the Zozosuit to take 3-D scans of customers' bodies. They use the measurements to recommend sizes and sell clothes such as suits, jeans, and T-shirts made from precut patterns. Orders are sent out within two weeks. Masahiro Ito, a board member who oversees engineering at the firm, says the fashion industry has not yet adapted to meet the needs of a generation accustomed to buying everything online, to their specifications, and at their convenience. "We offer exactly that," he says.[1] The company's continued success will depend on whether it can make its clothing affordable, a key concern for millennials. We will cover the topic of personalization and cost in chapter 4. However, unlike many retailers in the United States and Japan, Zozotown has taken steps to address personalization, one of the millennials' needs.

Thinking about (or finding out!) the answers to the following questions will give you a sense of how likely your company is to be disrupted.

- How well do your company's products or services address customer needs?

- How effective is your company in selling to both baby boomers and millennials?

Your answers to these questions will indicate how focused on customers your company really is. It's not technology or innovation from your competition that will disrupt your business; it's your customers. If you're not focused on them, they will leave as soon as they find a viable alternative, and their departure is only a matter of time.

FOCUS ON CUSTOMER NEEDS, NOT WHAT'S ARTICULATED

Understanding customers' needs is the first and most crucial step in dealing with disruption, and many companies don't try hard enough to reach that understanding. They focus on what their customers tell them they want. As Steve Jobs said, "Some people say, 'Give the customers what they want.' But that's not my approach. Our job is to figure out what they're going to want before they do. I think Henry Ford once said, 'If I'd asked customers what they wanted, they would have told me, *A faster horse!*' People don't know what they want until you show it to them. That's why I never rely on market research. Our task is to read things that are not yet on the page."[2]

Not everyone can be as brilliant (or as lucky) as Jobs was in doing this, but any company that tries can understand what's driving customers' statements, and companies that don't do this will fail. Companies have to figure out the drives behind the needs and think outside the box to meet them.

Take for example Jobs's approach to the iPhone. Other mobile phone companies reacted to customers' need for internet connectivity by trying to duplicate their desktop experience. But that didn't work on their phones' small screens. Jobs saw a new way to give customers what they wanted (connectivity)—make the screen bigger *and* create apps. The iPhone was so radically different that Steve Ballmer, the Microsoft CEO, dismissed it, saying, "There's no chance that the iPhone is going to get any significant market share. No chance. It's a $500 subsidized item. They may make a lot of money. But if you actually take a look at the 1.3 billion phones that get sold, I'd prefer to have our software in 60 percent or 70 percent or 80 percent of them, than I would have 2 percent or 3 percent, which is what Apple might get."[3] Other competitors dismissed the iPhone, too.

But customers loved the iPhone. Apple's revenue increased from $38 billion in 2008 to $229 billion in 2017. Most of the growth came from the iPhone. As figure 2 shows, the iPhone's contribution to Apple revenue increased from 5% to 62%. Most other handset manufacturers went out of business within four to seven years, except for Samsung, which unabashedly copied iPhone features. Though Ballmer later regretted his comment, Microsoft eventually withdrew its Windows Phone, and as of 2018, it has no presence in the smartphone market.

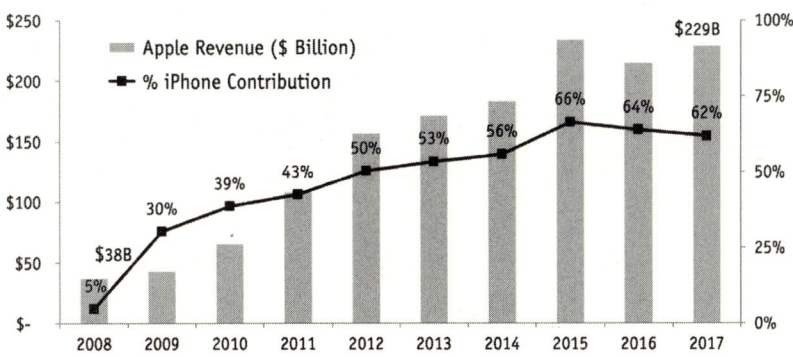

FIGURE 2 Apple revenue trends and iPhone contribution. Source: "Financial Information: Earnings Releases and 10K Annual Reports," Apple Investor Relations, https://goo.gl/1tqAi6.

RECOGNIZE THAT CUSTOMER NEEDS VARY BY COUNTRY AND GEOGRAPHY

In the past, American companies could count on people all over the world wanting the same products that their American customers wanted. The typical American company's strategy for overseas sales was to take what they were selling in the United States, make small packaging modifications, and sell it worldwide. At one time, customers in emerging markets were fine with that, since the U.S. brands were better than local ones. But the old approach to selling U.S. products in developing markets doesn't work anymore. The customers in developing markets are demanding products that are more suited to their own cultures and tastes. Multinationals aren't catering to these needs and thus are losing market share to domestic players.

To deal with disruption, you have to understand customers in your own county *and* you have to recognize that customers in different countries have different needs and figure out how to meet those. For example, a few years ago, customers in developing markets were looking for devices that provide connectivity on the go, but they couldn't afford what Apple and Samsung offered—and they didn't care about some of the fancy features. Global sales of smartphones priced below $200 increased from 35% in 2013 to 47% in 2017. Apple and Samsung didn't understand this and kept trying to sell the phones their American customers loved. That strategy didn't work. Starting in 2015, most new iPhones were priced at over $500 (see figure 3).

This gave Chinese manufacturers their opportunity. Chinese handset manufacturers, like Huawei, started creating the smartphones that customers in developing markets wanted. Their phones have such strong reception that calls could be made from basements and parking garages. OPPO focused on selling cheaper phones in rural China. Vivo, the second-largest smartphone manufacturer in China, focused on cameras in a market that's obsessed with selfies. Xiaomi had a smaller share and concentrated on selling high-end phones at a lower cost. Once these companies perfected their phones in China, they took them to other developing markets and to Europe. By 2018, Huawei had surpassed Apple.

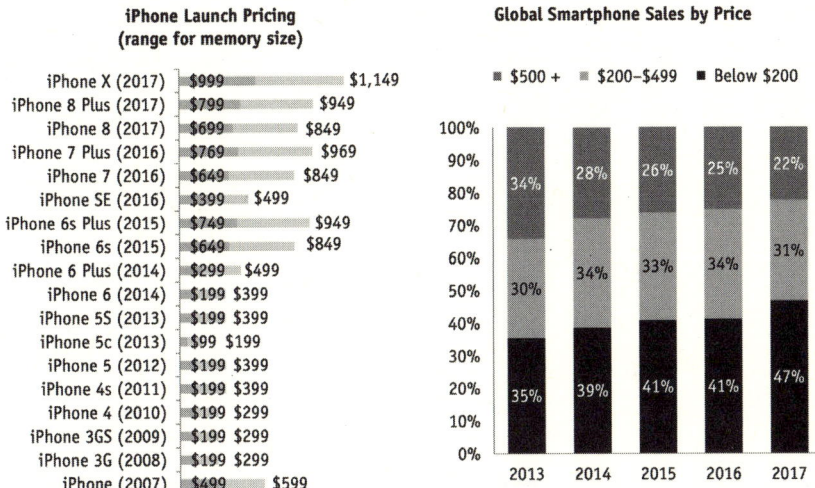

FIGURE 3 iPhone pricing and global smartphone sales, by price range. Sources: Jamie McKane, "How the Price of an iPhone Has Changed Over the Past 10 Years," Mybroadband, September 15, 2017, https://goo.gl/HsCLtM; Timothy W. Martin and Eric Bellman, "Samsung Joins Race to the Bottom for Global Smartphone Prices," *Wall Street Journal*, September 4, 2018, https://goo.gl/Do3yRU.

Chinese manufacturers won in developing markets because they were price competitive and focused on local needs—and not only in China. A little-known Chinese company, Transsion Holdings, captured a 40% share in African countries by offering four SIM slots to avoid out-of-network calls, a battery life of fifteen days, and a camera that's tuned to darker skin tones.[4] Combined global market share of Apple and Samsung declined, from 49% in the first quarter of 2013 to 33% in the second quarter of 2018, while Chinese manufacturers increased market share from 4% to 34% in the same time period (see figure 4).

According to Counterpoint Technology, most of the world's smartphone sales growth in the first quarter of 2017 was driven by India, the Middle East, and Africa. Chinese smartphones made up half of India's sales in 2017, compared to 15% a year earlier. Xiaomi had the same market share as the leader, Samsung. Apple's response? They began manufacturing the older-generation iPhone SE in India, without modifying

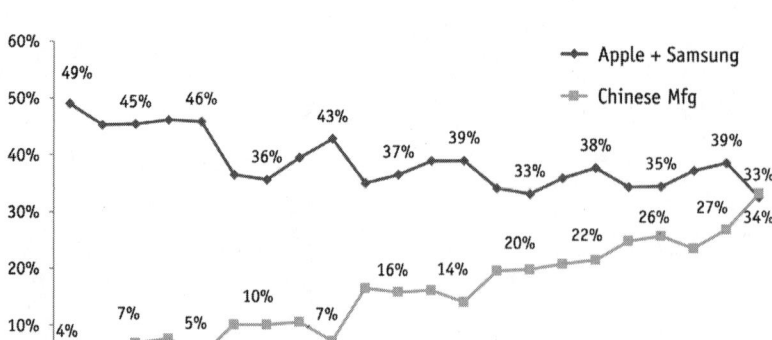

FIGURE 4 Global smartphone market share of Apple and Samsung compared to Chinese manufacturers, including Huawei, Xiaomi, and Oppo. Source: "Global Market Share Held by Leading Smartphone Vendors from 4th Quarter 2009 to 4th Quarter 2018," Statistica, January 2019, https://goo.gl/2DxEzK.

it in any way for the needs of the Indian market. Needless to say, sales were low. And the Chinese are gaining market share in Europe, too. As of the first quarter of 2018, they have 25% of the European market. According to the research firm Canalys, Samsung and Apple sales are declining while Huawei and Xiaomi sales are soaring.[5]

The same sort of thing is happening all over the world in consumer goods, fast food, telecom, and banking—local companies are gaining market share, multinationals are losing it. Multinationals' old copy-and-paste strategy for selling their products and services abroad doesn't work anymore. If multinationals fail to cater to local needs, not only will they lose customers abroad but also their competitors will develop products and sell them in the West and in developing markets. Chinese smartphone manufacturers like Xiaomi and OnePlus are making an effort to enter the United States, despite significant U.S. opposition to Huawei.[6]

GENERATIONAL CHANGES WILL DRIVE FUTURE DISRUPTIONS

While local companies are taking market share away from multinationals, generational changes are accelerating the process, both in emerging markets and in the West. This is because some products from emerging markets are attractive to younger generations worldwide, and in all countries, baby boomers are downsizing. This is a huge change for most corporations, which are structured around selling to boomers and must now learn to sell to younger generations.

Even Apple sells the iPhone by focusing on features like larger screens, OLED glass, facial recognition, and faster processors. These may appeal to boomers, but they mean nothing to millennials and Gen Z. If companies want to stay in business, they need to figure out what *would* have meaning to millennials and Gen Z. I like my iPhone, but my Gen Z daughter loves all the ways she can personalize her Android phone. Like many in her generation, she is into photography and can fine-tune her Android phone far better than she could fine-tune an iPhone. Different things appeal to different generations, and companies have been slow to understand this and to develop products and services that reflect it.

The following will briefly summarize the broad buying habits of different generations and discuss (in very broad terms) what companies need to do to retain or attract them.

Baby Boomers

Baby boomers, born between 1945 and 1963, have long been the powerhouse behind the U.S. economy, accounting for half of all U.S. spending.[7] Boomers buy an estimated 50% of the computers and 66% of the cars sold in the United States. They grew up during an economic boom and, despite the Great Recession, some still enjoy the benefits of decades of stock market growth. Boomers believe in brand names and credentials and will spend more on products, services, and employees that have them. For example, the blind application of Six Sigma principles in areas like research and development (R&D) proved disastrous.[8] This reliance on the known and the proven is one reason that boomer executives struggle with new business models, ideas, and diversity.

In many ways, boomers are different from previous generations. They are living longer, retiring later, carrying more debt (including student loans for their children and sometimes even grandchildren), and maintaining discretionary spending. They like to travel, visit family members, take a cruise, or tour foreign destinations. And, as they age, they spend more on health care, pets, and home. Although they like to shop in-store, they are comfortable with online purchases, too. As the generation ages, they are spending more time watching TV. They are more open to traditional TV, newspaper ads, and celebrity endorsements.

In general, companies are adept at selling to this group, although it would benefit boomer executives to become more open to new ideas instead of relying upon what has worked in the past. For example, they would serve their companies and customers better if they relied more on personalization and flexibility than on scale and lowering unit costs. Relying on old ways of doing things and expecting different results doesn't work.

Generation X

Generation X, born from the mid-1960s to the early 1980s, is smaller in size than the boomers or the millennials, and in many ways they are like the neglected middle child when it comes to marketing efforts— few campaigns are directed solely at them. They exhibit characteristics of both boomers and millennials. On the one hand, they are comfortable with technology and respond well to personalized offers tailored to their interests. On the other hand, they love loyalty programs and typically buy from stores for which they have loyalty cards. They also are loyal to their favorite brands. They spend money on travel and luxury products.

Gen X shoppers are more down to earth and are less likely than boomers to be influenced by fashion trends. Maybe because many grew up in divorced families, maybe because many came of age during a recession, they tend to be more cynical and streetwise than boomers. Though Gen Xers are as brand loyal as baby boomers, they heavily research online before buying and then stick with their choices. Gen X loves to eat out (as do millennials), but they will also use coupons and, like boomers, will cook at home.[9]

Millennials

Millennials were born from the early 1980s to the mid-1990s and now outnumber the boomers. Millennials grew up with technology and are very comfortable with it. They have high levels of student debt, and the Great Recession had a disproportionate impact on their finances. With less money to spend, they are putting off commitments such as marriage and home ownership. Many of them are unable to afford their own apartments and still live with their parents.[10]

Once you understand that millennials have less disposable income than other generations and like to express their individuality, you begin to understand their most important needs and basic buying habits. They are reluctant to buy items such as cars, luxury goods, or music. Instead, they prefer to use services that provide access to products without the burdens of ownership—think of Spotify. Their preferences gave rise to the so-called sharing economy. When it comes to retail, millennials value the quality of their shopping experience over specific brands and products. Though millennials don't have the same coffee fixation as baby boomers, they do love Starbucks (despite the prices!), because they enjoy the whole experience of being there.[11]

Millennials check reviews and compare prices on their smartphones while shopping, rather than buying by brand. They listen more to their peers than to celebrities. They are more comfortable with online shopping than most boomers are. However, although they are price sensitive, they still value quality—and are willing to take the time to look for it at an affordable price. Younger millennials will buy at stores because they love personalized services and are willing to pay for them.

Millennials of all ages are seriously into wellness. They exercise more, buy healthy foods to prepare at home and choose them when eating out, and smoke less than previous generations. You are more likely to find them at a farmers' market than in a grocery aisle.[12] They also are socially conscious and value companies that put purpose over profit.

The values of millennials are similar across the globe. Japanese millennials don't drink, don't drive, and don't spend a crazy number of hours in the office.[13] They don't even buy wristwatches—they use their smartphones. They are not into the things that their parents considered sacrosanct. They prefer a simple lifestyle and they're thrifty, whether they're buying cosmetics or hotel rooms. Japanese millennials, in short, are like U.S. millennials and millennials the world over—they want value for their yen, like their peers all over the world.

Generation Z

Generation Z is now the largest generation in the United States, and the most diverse. They were born between 1995 and the mid-2000s and thus grew up with technology. They don't trust large corporations or brands, but the Great Recession didn't impact Gen Z, so they focus less on price than millennials do.[14] But, in many ways, those in Gen Z are millennials on steroids.

Gen Zers are less likely to go to college than Gen Xers and millennials —they want to avoid racking up education-related debt. They thus are more entrepreneurial and less likely to work for large corporations.[15] They are more socially sophisticated than other generations and more skillful than boomers in using the media. Many of them are rebels with a cause, and their social and media skills make them more effective in their rebellion than, say, the boomers were. And those in Gen Z may disrupt higher education and corporations more thoroughly than the millennials have.

HOW GENERATIONAL CHANGES AFFECT BUSINESSES

All these shifts in the population and changing demographics have of course changed customer needs, and this is a big challenge for most businesses. Few large corporations know how to research Gen Z, let alone reach them with advertising. Changing tastes that companies didn't anticipate are disrupting entire industries.

For example, millennials' preference for healthy food has completely disrupted the food and beverage industry. Millennials value—and will pay for—organic, natural, sustainable, and locally sourced food. Packaged food sales are decreasing while sales of healthier, fresher foods are increasing. Major food giants—Kraft, Kellogg's, Mondelez, and the Campbell's Soup Company—are struggling.[16] Because they failed to react to these changing needs, their revenues have declined significantly. And ever since the links between sugar and obesity—and companies' cover-ups—have come to light, millennials have been shunning sugary drinks. Even industry giants like Pepsi and Coca-Cola have seen declines in revenues.

Companies in the food and beverage industry are trying to reduce costs with mergers and acquisitions. They're replacing top executives; General Mills, Hershey's, and Mondelez all named new CEOs. Now the conflict is brewing between retailers and food companies. Retailers are reducing shelf space for packaged foods and increasing aisle space for fresher foods. The industry is caught in a vortex and is struggling to find a way out.

If you want to avoid disruption, focus on the new generations and their new needs. The longer you wait, the harder it will be for you catch up. Keep up with the generational changes in all markets or you will be left behind.

REALIZING THAT TECHNOLOGY AND INNOVATION DO NOT DISRUPT COMPANIES

Most people attribute disruption to technology, thinking of the iPhone, 3-D printing, robotics, and artificial intelligence. However, technology alone does not cause disruption. The iPhone didn't succeed because of its technology. The iPhone's technology came from Nokia, which sued Apple for infringing on its patents. (Apple settled.) The iPhone succeeded because it met customer needs better than any other product at the time did. If we're all driving electric cars in five years, we will point to Tesla's technology as disruptive—yet, according to Wikipedia, the electric car was invented in 1834. Customer needs and demand, even if practically subconscious at times, are the real source of disruption. Electric car technology was not disruptive in 1834, or even in 1934, because customers didn't want it.

Realizing that technology and innovation do not disrupt markets but merely enable solutions is the fourth step in dealing with disruption. Technology is only a means to an end. Customers' needs have driven every past marketplace disruption, and they will drive future disruptions, too. The technology and innovation that deliver on customer needs will be adopted; technologies that don't—no matter how innovative they are—will be discarded. Yet blindly investing in technology, thinking it will save them and their organizations, is a mistake too many leaders make.

The only way leaders can avoid disruption is by focusing their attention on customers, figuring out what they need, and investing only in technologies or innovations that serve those needs. Only by accepting such realities can leaders cheat death and keep their companies alive.

DISCONNECT BETWEEN CUSTOMER NEEDS AND TECHNOLOGY DEVELOPMENT

When facing disruption, some leaders grab onto new technologies as a drowning person clutches a straw. They actually believe that inventing the next new gadget in their field will revive their declining revenues. So they invest in technology without focusing on customer needs.

Much of this false reliance on technology and innovation is motivated by business research, such as Stanford Business School's 2017 report on technological innovation and total wealth.[17] They analyzed eighty-five years' worth of patents and concluded that companies with the most patents experienced the most growth. If this is true, then how did IBM—which has more patents than any company in the world—lose its market share and decline so much in revenue? IBM filed 8,023 patents in 2016—an increase of 7.8% from 2015. Yet its revenue declined in both 2016 and 2017. The other companies on Stanford's top 10 list—including Canon and General Electric (GE)—are also struggling. The report—like most corporate leaders—doesn't understand that innovation is just a means to an end. Filing patents doesn't guarantee success. You can only grow by focusing on customer needs and then investing in technologies that deliver on those needs.

Examples abound. Look at car companies' investment in electric and self-driving technology. Customers are looking for fast, affordable, and safe transportation. The need hasn't changed much over the years, except that customers are additionally asking that their cars be less polluting. Though cars have to meet minimum safety and pollution standards, customers have choices between speed and affordability. They have the option of dedicated transportation, ride-sharing, or public transportation. Of course, a faster ride is more expensive.

The most significant constraint, even for a supposedly faster ride, is the road network and congestion, not vehicle speed. Flying taxis could address customers' need for a faster ride or commute better than all three of these, since flying removes dependence on roads or congestion. However, none of the car companies in the United States are investing in this technology—even though flying taxis are already being tested in Dubai (you can watch them on CNN and YouTube). They are being developed by Boeing, Airbus, and start-ups. The challenge is to make them affordable. However, due to Federal Aviation Administration regulations, we may see them introduced in Dubai, Japan, or Europe before they appear in the United States.[18]

Instead of investigating and investing in a technology that seems poised to meet customers' needs, car companies are pursuing electric and self-driving cars, which don't get people to their destinations any faster but are likely to be more expensive—and to have other problems, too. Autonomous vehicles have significant safety issues. Waymo, Google's autonomous vehicle company, is reinstalling safety drivers behind the wheel. *Scientific American* says that electric cars are not necessarily clean and battery-powered vehicles are only as green as the electricity supplier.[19] Electric vehicles merely move pollution from cities to rural utilities, and the level of pollution will not be reduced unless utilities start using renewable energy sources. These technologies are unlikely to be the game changers that they are made out to be, and lukewarm customer demand is an early indicator of that.

So why are car companies still investing in autonomous cars and electric cars but not in flying taxis? It's partly because they've fallen for the buzz created by Tesla (for electric cars) and Google (for autonomous vehicles). It's partly their fear of regulations. And it's partly that they remain too focused on investors, who have fallen for the buzz, too, and think their stock prices will go down if the car companies don't invest in these technologies. But the fact is that car companies will be disrupted if customers find better options elsewhere. Flying taxis—with their entirely new way of addressing customer needs—could do to the auto industry what the iPhone did to the smartphone industry. The same sort of thing could occur in all industries—from pharmaceuticals to financial services to cable. Companies that invest in technologies and innovations that address customer needs will be successful; those that invest in technology for its own sake will fail, despite the billions of dollars they've spent.

WALMART VERSUS AMAZON

Big companies are failing, creating economic uncertainty and job insecurity, because they aren't focusing on customers. This is as true for companies that serve end users as for those that serve other businesses. All businesses get disrupted, no matter how far downstream in the supply chain they may be. If you ignore customer needs, your company will be disrupted—and the longer you've delayed disruption's impact, the greater its damage will be.

When business leaders understand and address their customers' needs—including the different needs of different generations and cultures—their companies succeed. When they don't, their companies get disrupted. As Sam Walton, the founder of Walmart, famously said, "There is only one boss—the customer. And he can fire everybody in the company from the chairman on down, simply by spending his money somewhere else."

Walton focused on high-volume products, kept prices low, and revolutionized the retail industry. His company has more revenue and has employed more people than any other company in the world. Because of Walton's conviction about the importance of his customers, you would expect Walmart to have the best customer service rating, too. Ironically, the American Customer Satisfaction Index consistently gives Walmart the lowest customer service rating of any retail store.[20] It's no surprise that Walmart is now failing—not because of Amazon but because their customers are choosing to buy somewhere else. This is happening to companies across industries, including GE, IBM, P&G, and Hewlett-Packard. They once were leaders; now they are being disrupted.

The reason, in nearly all cases, is their lack of customer focus. That is the recipe for disruption, especially now, as customers are becoming ever more informed and ever less loyal. Your talk of innovation will not sway them. Advertising will not sway them. Only when your products and services address their needs will even your old customers buy from you. It's ironic that although Sam Walton understood this so well, his heirs don't seem to get it. And thus their company, once the leading corporation in the United States, is steadily losing customers while Amazon—with its unwavering focus on customer needs—is gaining customers and seems poised to continue to do so. Is your company more like Walmart or Amazon in its customer focus and willingness to embrace change?

2

CUSTOMER-FOCUSED STRATEGIES NEEDED TO AVOID DISRUPTION

T O AVOID DISRUPTION, IT'S not enough to understand customer needs—you have to devise strategies to address them. Too many leaders focus instead on investors and increasing short-term stock prices. Of course, companies must increase long-term shareholder value. But the way to do that is not through short-term, investor-focused strategies but by longer-term strategies for keeping customers happy.

Most leaders understand that they have to deliver what customers need, but their companies' incentives and compensation don't support that and their short tenure exacerbates the need for short-term performance. Most U.S. executives are rewarded with excessive stock awards and stock options with two to three years' vesting and ten years' exercise, as figure 5 shows. Most of these are awarded based on financial metrics.

Naturally, leaders focus on strategies that maximize their compensation (stock prices), even when doing so directly conflicts with delivering to customers in the long term. Some of the ways in which leaders increase short-term stock prices (and their own compensation) are mergers and acquisitions, incremental innovation, marketing, lobbying, and global expansion. But short-term strategies like these all too often have disastrous long-term consequences, as customers end up disrupting the company and industry. The *New York Times* reported that blue chip companies that used cheap debt to acquire other companies were in trouble.[1] Strategies that incentivize leaders based on the long-term value they create are a better bet.

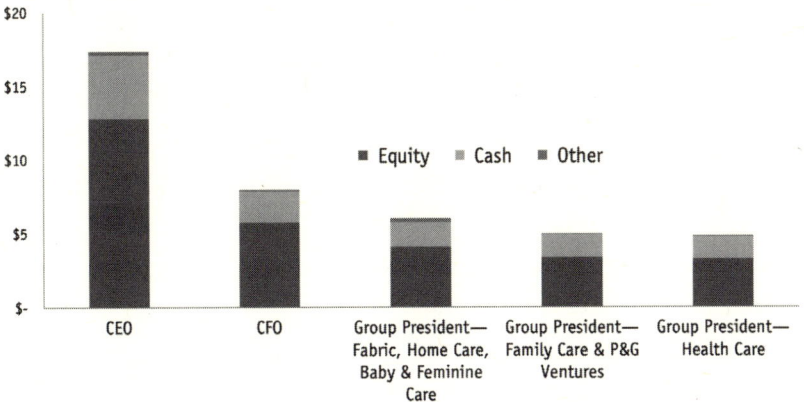

FIGURE 5 P&G leadership compensation (in millions). *Cash* includes salary and bonuses, *equity* includes stock and option awards, and *other* includes retirement plans, executive benefits, and other income. On an average 70% of P&G executive compensation came from equity (20% of that was stock options). Source: Procter & Gamble Company, "2018 Proxy Statement," August 24, 2018, https://goo.gl/faahkg.

Tying leaders' compensation to metrics like customer feedback on social media, repeat customer rate, and growth in the user base could get leaders focused on customers. This should be balanced with financial metrics. With their compensation dependent upon customer satisfactions, leaders would devise strategies that deliver on customer need and truly harness the power of their organization behind them.

Consider Procter & Gamble, a 185-year-old American consumer goods company, which is now struggling because it followed short-term strategies like the ones mentioned instead of long-term strategies devised to meet their customer's changing needs. And this despite the fact that P&G's purpose, values, and principles statement says, "We will provide branded products and services of superior quality and value that improve the lives of the world's consumers, now and for generations to come."[2] P&G just doesn't seem to understand that markets are changing all over the world and that what worked for them in the past will not work now.

Only a few companies are more customer focused than Procter & Gamble, and its long life is a testament to that. Nevertheless, its revenue declined from $83 billion in 2014 to $67 billion in 2018, as figure 6 shows. It tried to increase profitability by getting rid of unprofitable brands in 2016 and 2017. However, this approach doesn't seem to be working, as margin again declined in 2017—even with the best and brightest doing its advertising and R&D.

Why aren't P&G's old strategies working now? Despite the growing economy, U.S. shoppers have been cutting back on household goods, and P&G's organic growth has stalled at between 1% and 3%. While subsidiary Gillette has lost market share in the United States, Dollar Shave Club and Harry's are grabbing it. In India, P&G is losing market share to companies that deliver more natural, traditional Indian products, as Patanjali does. Millennials everywhere care more than previous generations about having healthy, natural products, but they won't pay high prices for those products. As Nelson Peltz, activist investor, puts it, "Customer preferences are changing worldwide." All this means big losses, and P&G leaders don't seem to understand the reasons for it.[3]

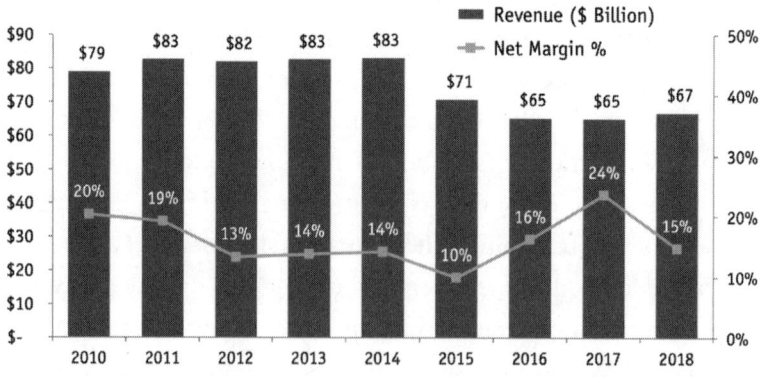

FIGURE 6 Procter & Gamble revenue and profit margin trends. Source: "Annual Reports," Procter & Gamble, https://goo.gl/5KEp6V.

To summarize Peltz, one of those reasons is that millennials don't trust big brands and prefer natural, organic wellness products.[4] In essence, P&G's strategy of incrementally improving its existing products and launching at higher price points every year, and relying on advertising to keep customers buying, doesn't work with millennials. The company seems to be losing its ability to grow quickly and to increase prices, actions that made them an investor darling in the past. To survive, P&G must come up with strategies that address millennials' needs for natural and organic products. This is what Patanjali, the Indian upstart, did—and doing it too could put P&G back on a growth path and create long-term investor value.

Understanding customer needs, coming up with strategies to address them, and then aligning operational, organizational structure and incentives around them is the recipe for success. Very few companies are doing this well now. Leaders who win will stop focusing on short-term strategies for investors and will make customers their first priority. Only then can they choose the strategies that lead to success and align their entire organizations around them.

How likely is your company to succeed? Thoughtful answers to the following questions will give you a good sense of that.

- How well does your company focus on and understand your customers?
- How effective are the strategies and capabilities your company has embraced to deliver on customer needs?

The better your company is at doing both, the more likely it is to grow. Even if your company is small, you are well prepared to take on industry leaders if you keep an eye on changing customer needs. And if you keep revising your strategies to meet those needs, you'll keep growing. The worse you are doing in terms of these questions, the more you need to bring the focus back to customers and embrace strategies that deliver on customer needs. Otherwise, you will be disrupted.

WHY COMPANIES DON'T FOCUS ON CUSTOMERS

You could trace the source of most behavior to incentives. When leaders' compensation is based on short-term stock price performance, that's what they focus on, even if doing so means terrible customer experiences and long-term disaster. An MIT study found that CEO and leadership compensation tilted toward stock grants and options starting in the early 1970s.[5] Since then, executive pay has rarely been tied to customer satisfaction, customer feedback, or any other metric focusing on customers.

When entrepreneurs start a company, they know their success—including their venture capital—is tied directly to customer acceptance, so, naturally, pleasing customers is their focus. But as companies grow, investors tie executive compensation to short-term share price growth. That's how Tesla proposed compensating Elon Musk—according to market valuation or share price growth, with no mention of customers. Though the implicit assumption is that Musk will have to get customer acceptance to grow the company, the reality is different. Musk is battling with Tesla's short sellers instead of focusing on customers.[6]

History shows that increasing incentives too much can lead to bad behavior. Wells Fargo compromised on customer trust to improve stock valuation. GE spent $24 billion on stock buybacks between 2016 and 2017 to increase its share prices, and got into a cash crunch in 2018.[7] When executives focus on short-term stock prices, the long-term health of the business suffers. Firing everyone in top management and replacing them with entrepreneurs is not the solution. Even entrepreneurs like Mark Zuckerberg seem to lose focus on their customers when their companies go public. Incentives, organization structure, culture, hiring, and training have to be changed to bring an organization's focus back to customers, and that shift has to start at the top, with how executives are incentivized.

Investors win in the long run when customers are happy, because their long-term gains are tied to continuing customer satisfaction. Ask any small business owner. Small business owners know that their survival depends on their ability to keep customers happy. Some large companies have shown that concentrating on customer needs is good for the shareholders; the two interests are tightly linked in the long term. Customer-pleasing strategies are not always immediately profitable, however. For example, Amazon lost money with its Prime service at first, though in the long term the program pleased both investors and customers. If the company had concentrated on short-term profits, Amazon would probably not be where it is today.

And if executive compensations are linked to short-term profits, neither customers nor shareholders will be satisfied. This is why CEO pay, too, should be linked to customer satisfaction and the company's long-term growth. Studies show that as companies become more prominent, leaders become more distant from customers. They spend more time managing the organization and investors, less time with customers. They believe their role ends with training employees. A 2017 HBR survey of one thousand CEOs found that, on average, CEOs spend 10% of their time with clients, 7% with suppliers, and the rest with internal groups. Unless you are a big customer, you will not get any attention from the CEO or his/her leadership team. The C-suite is very isolated from its customers—at companies that ultimately fail. The GE turnaround plan proposed by outgoing CEO John Flannery is a good example. The document is focused on investors and touts internal capabilities. There is no mention of gaining customer trust or addressing customer needs.[8]

Great leaders make time for their customers and learn from customer interactions. Hamdi Ulukaya, the Chobani CEO, stands outside the SoHo store to listen to his customers. The same is true for small business owners; they know that you can't run a small business while hiding in a back office. To lead a thriving company, the CEO has to spend time with customers. Otherwise, the company can't become customer focused. Training employees and changing the mission statement don't change the company's focus. Only CEOs who meet with customers, make them a priority, and understand them from their own direct experience can champion the change and carry others along with them.

FAILURE OF CURRENT BUSINESS STRATEGIES

It's no surprise that leaders devise investor-focused business strategies—that's what they think will maximize their compensation and provide job security. So they use strategies like incrementally improving products, marketing and advertising, mergers and acquisitions, global expansion, and special interests to reduce customer choices while (they hope) growing revenue and profit in the short term. These strategies aren't even meant to address current customer needs, let alone those of new customers, but to increase short-term stock prices. Retooling or refocusing these strategies on customer needs doesn't help either. Companies must abandon these losing strategies. They frustrate customers and ultimately lead to disruption. Let's review these no-win strategies and show how they fail to connect with customer needs.

Incremental Innovation

Companies spend a lot of money incrementally improving their existing products—even in the face of evidence that customers don't want them—to increase short-term revenue and profit. They launch "new and improved" household goods or automobiles with added features, every year, at higher price points. The goal is to extract as much money from customers as possible, as frequently as possible. Think of the incremental innovation to the iPhone that Apple launches each year. Investors love these upgrades, as they increase short-term company revenue and profitability, but the additional value for customers is minimal. Customers will eventually stop buying, and disrupters will then have their opportunity to enter the market.

For example, when P&G acquired Gillette in 2005, it increased the number of blades in the razor and raised its price every few years. Online razor companies such as Dollar Shave Club, Harry's (in 2011), and Edgewell Personal Care (in 2015) moved into the market, attracting customers with both cheaper blades and home delivery. Starting in 2013, Gillette's volume stopped growing, and it declined by 3% in 2016 and a further 2% in 2017.[9] To compensate for this declining volume,

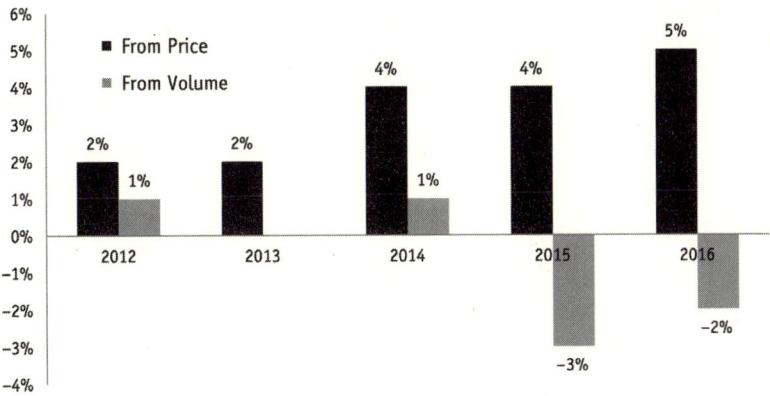

FIGURE 7 Gillette revenue increase—price versus volume. Source: Euromonitor, embedded figure, in Sharon Terlep, "Gillette, Bleeding Market Share, Cuts Prices of Razors," *Wall Street Journal*, April 4, 2017, https://goo.gl/fcxj86.

P&G increased prices by 4% in 2014 and in 2015, and by 5% in 2016 (figure 7). Gillette finally realized that even higher-end customers have their spending limits. So P&G cut prices in 2017 and launched new products at price points closer to those of their online rivals, trying to win back their customers. But the customers did not return.

The incremental innovation strategy is still used across industries. Based on our work with clients, we estimate that companies spend 20% of their R&D budget on breakthrough innovation and 80% on incremental innovation, despite the fact that breakthrough innovation is far more likely to address customer needs and thus to grow revenue and profit. Think about what the first iPhone did for Apple. Companies keep spending on incremental innovation, thinking it will assure a return on investment, but that is not true anymore. That strategy worked with baby boomers and Gen X. But it doesn't work with millennials, who don't value incremental innovation and won't pay for new features they may never use. Samsung has started including more technology in its midpriced and lower-priced smartphones, instead of only in its flagship brands, to attract millennials.[10]

Instead of incrementally improving products, companies should be spending their R&D money on finding better ways to meet customer needs. If they don't, someone else will—and probably at a lower price. For example, automotive companies kept launching cars at higher prices, claiming they had increased safety and better met emission requirements. Many millennials responded by using ride-hailing, and convincing them to change their lifestyles and buy cars will be difficult. Now other generations have caught up with the trend. As their night vision fades, boomers are using ride-hailing services to avoid driving in the dark. Gen Xers use them as designated drivers.

Marketing and Advertising

Businesses across industries spend a significant amount of money on marketing and advertising to convince customers to buy their products or services. They believe that advertising can convince customers to choose their products over their competitors' products. Investors, too, believe in advertising—they think brand recognition means long-term value. That may once have been true, but it isn't now, for two reasons.

First, millennials trust peer reviews far more than advertising and brands. They don't believe ads, and they don't value celebrity or third-party endorsements.[11] And across generations, people simply are seeing and watching fewer ads. They use ad blockers online and various devices to avoid ads on cable. Many don't even have cable, so TV ads are reaching fewer and fewer people. Even major events like the Super Bowl, the Oscars, and the Olympics have smaller audiences each year. When viewers are forced to suffer through ads, many choose to not watch at all.

In their desperation to catch customer attention, companies like Coca-Cola and Pepsi switched from advertising to in-store promotions and point-of-sale marketing—putting products near the checkout counter. Their logic was that if people saw the product while they were waiting to check out, they'd buy it impulsively, but that doesn't work as well as it once did, either. Customers are not looking around them;

they're on their smartphones. And the checkout lines aren't as long as they once were in many places. Knowing that customers won't wait, many retailers are making checkouts simpler.[12]

The golden age of marketing and advertising is over. Companies are wasting their money if they think they can convince customers to buy their products with ads. Millennials have always been brand agnostic, and Gen Xers and boomers see fewer ads than they once did—and trust them less.[13] Instead of spending money on advertising, companies should find ways to get genuine customer reviews that millennials and Gen Z will trust.

Many big companies realize this and have cut their marketing and advertising budgets. Many small and medium-sized companies fall for claims by Google and Facebook about their high return on investment on their ads. But without third-party validation, these claims mean nothing. P&G reduced online spending significantly, as their push for transparency revealed it was a waste of effort and money. Uber believed that their mobile ad agency (Fetch) was billing for fake clicks and filed a lawsuit.[14] So, companies must stop relying on advertising—including online advertising—to get customers to buy their products. It doesn't work.

Mergers and Acquisitions

When their core businesses become less popular, many companies acquire or merge with competitors to restrict customer choices and increase revenue and profits. For example, mergers among airlines has meant charges for baggage and higher fees, to compensate for falling ticket prices. Companies claim that these acquisitions improve their efficiency, and they don't mention customer needs. Wall Street expects mergers to increase profits due to lower overhead. But mergers are usually bad for both employees and customers. They mean layoffs—though usually head counts rise again later, in the form of temporary workers and outsourced vendors. Customers are the real losers.

For example, after all the mergers, airlines continue to charge higher and higher prices for additional services, to increase their revenue.

When customers don't have choices, they have to pay them, and in 80% of the air travel market, customers don't have choices beyond the big four—United, American, Delta, and Southwest. Mounting customer dissatisfaction with all this probably means that Congress will eventually act against current industry practices.[15]

Mergers and acquisitions no longer guarantee rising profits. Recognizing this trend, some companies are off-loading their acquisitions to remain competitive. Consider GE. Jack Welch grew the company, acquiring one thousand companies. But many GE units behaved like monopolies and twisted customers' arms to increase revenue and profit. Naturally, customer discontent brewed. Customers in the railroad industry complained that GE Rail (now GE Transportation) forced them to buy rail cars and hardware they didn't need. GE Rail even discouraged the sharing of customer-demand data with other railroads for smoother operations! As soon as they found viable alternatives, railroads moved away from GE.

Jeff Immelt, GE's next CEO, had to shed a dozen or more businesses that Welch had cobbled together. But he continued to acquire other companies to please investors and never focused on customers' needs. While utilities were moving from carbon-based fuel to renewable energy, Immelt was betting on coal and crude oil.

The next CEO, John Flannery, appointed in late 2017, decided to shrink GE to three businesses—aviation, health care, and energy/power—and get out of lighting, locomotives, and other businesses. But the focus is *still* on shareholder returns, and the company has not shared plans to gain customer confidence. GE's future does not look bright.

Mergers and acquisitions do not predict growth and profitability; they're signs that a company is struggling against disruption. This strategy works only if it helps companies meet customer needs, and even then, companies may end up paying more and taking drastic actions to keep investors happy. If a company does need new products and doesn't want to develop them, partnering with or licensing from companies that are pleasing their customers is a better strategy.

Global Expansion

Once, people in countries like China had a craze for American products, but now these people want products and services that cater to their needs. For example, China was once the largest market for KFC outside of the United States. The fad for American fried chicken ended, though; the Chinese eventually went back to dumplings. Unable to deliver those, KFC's parent company spun off its China business. KFC is not alone. According to the *Economist*, multinationals make less money outside of their home region than they once did.[16] These giants are not able to adapt quickly enough to changing customer needs, and local businesses are beating them in more and more markets. The writing is on the wall. Either U.S. companies cater to local needs or they lose the market.

Global expansion is not as simple as it once was. International trade will continue to increase, despite trade wars, but there are no virgin territories left for multinationals to enter. Even in markets where they are currently competing, they have to adapt to changing customer needs to be successful. If multinationals ignore the needs of customers in developing markets, a disrupter from these countries could end up disrupting U.S. or European markets. For example, as Amazon tries to enter China, U.S. grocery retailers are partnering with Alibaba, the Chinese e-commerce giant, to counter Amazon's acquisition of Whole Foods.

Lobbying and Special Interests

U.S. companies spend a lot of money lobbying federal, state, and local representatives to gain unfair market advantage and improve investor returns by restricting customer choices. The pharmaceutical industry, the biggest corporate spender on lobbying, has long opposed Medicare's and Medicaid's ability to negotiate drug pricing.[17] The United States is the only country in the world where government insurance providers are not allowed to negotiate drug pricing. It is also the only country where pharmaceutical prices are increasing rapidly. Despite the United States being the largest pharmaceutical market in the world, U.S. customers pay the highest drug prices anywhere in the world.

The government's restrictions on customer choices don't end at the federal level. There are restrictions imposed by state and local government as well. For example, customers in the United States can't buy cars directly from manufacturers because state franchise laws protect dealerships.

But customers are successfully pressuring their representatives to change laws. Despite significant resistance to ride-hailing from the taxi lobby, most cities yielded to local pressure and allowed ride-sharing. In most industries, it's only a matter of time. Either elected representatives will listen to their constituents or they will be voted out of office. Lobbying is not a sustainable strategy to increase investor returns. People all over the country are disgusted by it.

Not all lobbying is bad. It's essential for any business to spend money on educating lawmakers. But more money gets spent trying to influence lawmakers to restrict customer choices than on educating them. The money spent influencing lawmakers is counterproductive. Once company practices become public, it destroys their reputation with customers for good.

Different Strategies for Changing Demographics

It's time to stop relying on business strategies like those described here. All of these strategies focus too heavily on short-term stock prices and not on long-term growth. Businesses and leaders have to focus on serving their customers and must devise new strategies that will meet their customers' current and future needs. If they don't, customers will disrupt their businesses—more aggressively and more swiftly than they have in the past, too. This trend will only accelerate as millennials and Gen Z become the dominant buying groups.

NEW CUSTOMER-FOCUSED STRATEGIES ARE NEEDED TO AVOID DISRUPTION

Modifying those old strategies won't attract or keep customers. To meet customer needs now and in the future, companies have to develop new, customer-focused strategies. Some companies are already doing this and making a fortune.

Consider Chobani's explosive growth. Understanding that customers want healthy food and will pay twice as much for Greek yogurt, Chobani's founder, Hamdi Ulukaya, bought a dairy factory from Kraft.[18] Chobani immediately became popular with health-conscious customers. Instead of selling the company, Hamdi scaled quickly and catered to the growing demand. The company built a big warehouse across the road from its plant, and another big plant in Idaho. The ability to meet customers' growing demand for healthy food made Chobani grow. Its U.S. yogurt market share increased from 7% in 2010 to 22% in 2016, while Danone's and Yoplait's shares declined (figure 8). The company soon expanded into international markets.

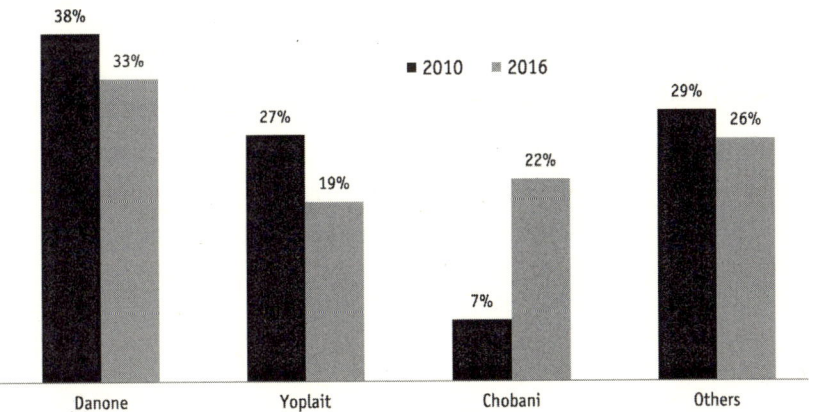

FIGURE 8 U.S. yogurt market share. Source: Euromonitor, embedded figure, in John Kell, "General Mills Loses the Culture Wars," *Fortune*, May 22, 2017, https://goo.gl/JfeRdQ.

The following is an overview of the strategies—service, personalization, speed, quality, and reinvention—that help companies deliver on customer needs. Subsequent chapters will detail how to use them.

Service

All customers love services such as warranties, faster returns, and easy credit. Many also love free shipping, help during shopping, easy checkout, and other services that benefit them. Most will spend more money when a company provides the services they value. But many companies don't do this well. To beat the competition, they offer services to all segments and then realize that they're not profitable. What works far better is targeting services to specific segments, which can do wonders in developing customer loyalty and increasing their spending. Amazon's Prime is a great example.

Personalization

Millennials' desire to express their individuality is already driving demand for personalization, for products and services that are tailored to each individual. However, companies struggle with this, too, because millennials are not willing to pay a premium price. Companies can make personalization affordable by thinking outside of the box about how to design, create or manufacture, and deliver products or services. A few companies, such as Zozotown, are experimenting with personalization, but no one has figured it out. It's a big opportunity and a threat for all businesses.

Speed

Millennials want everything now and are impatient about everything, from their careers to their purchases. They have little brand loyalty and will embrace other products or services if their old favorites don't show up on time. Either you adapt to this mind-set or you lose to companies that do. And it's not just millennials; older generations are getting impatient too. They don't like to wait at checkout counters or on the phone, and they won't wait for their favorite brands. So leaders must figure out how to deliver faster. Otherwise, before they know it, their customers will be buying from their competitors. And, for most business leaders, doing things faster means thinking in entirely new ways, in ways that match their customers' new expectations. Chobani is an excellent example of how companies can scale quickly when their products become a hit with customers. Fast fashion companies such as Zara show how companies can quickly respond to changing customer trends.

Quality

More and more customers are reading peer reviews on Amazon and other sites before buying products or services. They're looking at product performance, service, and quality issues, and they trust what their peers tell them—not companies' claims or advertising. Now, all products and services are judged according to how well they work for customers. Improving quality is a sure way of getting repeat business and attracting new customers with favorable reviews. Most leaders don't try hard enough for quality. As soon as they've beaten the competition, they consider their products good enough. But in today's world, no company—no matter how far ahead of the competition it is—stays good enough for long. You have to continue to improve quality to remain relevant. Aldi and Lidl have shown how a focus on quality made discount grocers popular throughout Europe.

Reinvention

Customer needs change, and it's difficult to predict what those needs will be in the future. Delighting current customers is not enough. You have to keep wowing them—and your new customers, too, whoever they may be. The only way to do that is to become skilled at creating strategies that support your customers' needs, and then to keep updating those strategies. This means setting up your whole organization to identify and respond to customers' needs as, and even before, they arise. Disney is an excellent example of a company that has changed itself over decades to remain relevant to all generations.

A crucial part of making these strategies successful is companies' ability to use their operations to deliver on customer needs. You can't do it with the Industrial Revolution–era operational philosophy of "Bigger is better" and "One size fits all." The only reason Chobani became successful is because of its ability to scale operations as customer demand increased. Hamdi said as much: "Never has a food aisle been challenged liked this and changed so quickly by a startup ever. Some say we're the fastest growing startup ever, including technology."[19]

Most companies don't do this as well as Chobani did. Tesla is struggling to increase its production for its Model 3 even as customers are rescinding their offers and buying competing products. Corporate leaders have long neglected operations. It's time to bring the focus back to them, too. In short, companies need to create strategies and operations to deliver on customer needs.

SUCCESSFUL TURNAROUNDS

Every company will fail at some point; what determines their survival is how quickly they get back on their feet. One of the most significant recoveries in the past twenty years is Apple. The Apple board of directors fired Steve Jobs in 1985, under pressure from CEO John Sculley. Jobs said:

> I didn't see it then, but it turned out that getting fired from Apple was the best thing that could have ever happened to me. The heaviness of being successful was replaced by the lightness of being a beginner again, less sure about everything. It freed me to enter into one of the most creative periods of my life. I'm pretty sure none of this would have happened if I hadn't been fired from Apple. It was awful-tasting medicine, but I guess the patient needed it. Sometimes life hits you in the head with a brick. Don't lose faith. I'm convinced the only thing that kept me going was that I loved what I did. You've got to find what you love.[20]

After leaving Apple, Jobs started NeXT and launched Pixar Animation Studios. During those years, Jobs the visionary evolved into Jobs the businessperson. Ironically, Apple struggled and wanted Jobs back. Jobs returned to Apple in 1997, where he focused on customer needs, making products that even grandmas can use. With innovations such as the iPod, iPhone, and iPad, he eventually turned the company around. And the rest, as they say, is history.

Apple is not the only impressive turnaround story. General Motors bounced back after its 2008 bankruptcy by improving the quality and safety of its cars. Marvel rediscovered itself after a 1990s bankruptcy when the comics market crashed. Now Iron Man, the Avengers, Spider-Man, and X-Men are billion-dollar franchises. These are just a few of the companies that have shown themselves able to recover from failure. They all did it by abandoning the old strategies designed to bring short-term profits to investors and embracing new ones focused on customers.

3

CUSTOMER-FOCUS STRATEGY 1: WIN WITH CURRENT CUSTOMERS BEFORE CHASING AFTER NEW ONES

CURRENT CUSTOMERS HAVE HIGHER revenue and profit potential than new customers. And if you meet their needs better than the competition, they'll buy more from you. Research shows that existing customers are far more profitable than new customers—five to twenty-five times more profitable.[1] New customers are expensive to acquire and typically produce less revenue once you do acquire them than satisfied current customers would. Yet, when faced with declining revenues, most companies focus on finding new customers. This is like pouring more water into a bucket with a hole in it. If your customers are draining away, fix the bucket first, or get a new one! But most companies just pour in more water.

Consider Walmart. They sell more goods and employ more people than any company in the world. They changed the retail landscape in the 1990s, but from 2012 to 2016, sales growth and profits steadily declined (see figure 9). Revenue growth declined from 6% in 2012 to −1% in 2016, while net income went from 4% to 3%. From 2017 to 2019 (estimated), revenue increased from 1% to 3%, while net income declined from 3% to 1%. Thus, while Walmart managed to grow sales, it did so at the cost of profit.

Walmart responded to dropping store revenue by cutting back on inventory and laying off workers. That made things worse: customers complained that they couldn't find the products they wanted. The

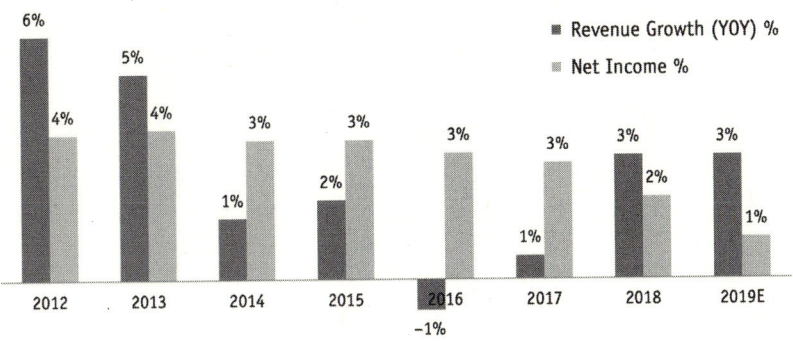

FIGURE 9 Walmart revenue and profit trends. Source: "Wal-Mart Stores, Inc.: Revenues and Sales," eMarketer Retail, https://goo.gl/VqndAt.

layoffs lowered morale, so employees refused to engage and answer simple questions from customers. Industry analysts routinely reported that customers were complaining about Walmart's poor selection, long checkout lines, and bad customer service.[2] Of course, some of the customers took their business to Amazon.

Instead of analyzing what the real problem was and trying to fix it, Walmart decided to seek new markets in e-commerce. They blamed Amazon for their declining revenue and customer dissatisfaction. Although they did address some employee complaints and a few customer issues, they focused on expanding Walmart's e-commerce, acquiring Jet.com in 2016 for $3 billion and buying brands such as Bonobos, ModCloth, and Moosejaw.

Walmart also introduced free two-day shipping for online orders over $35 for 2 million items, in January 2017, but unlike Amazon Prime, they didn't charge a yearly fee. Not surprisingly, without that, this idea lost the company a lot of money. From 2017 to 2019 (estimated), Walmart did grow its online revenue as a percentage of total revenue from 3.2% to 4.7%, but profit margin declined rapidly, from 2.8% to 1.0% (see figure 10). The exact impact of Walmart's online sales increase on profitability is difficult to decipher. Nevertheless, e-commerce has not been a positive contributor to their bottom line.

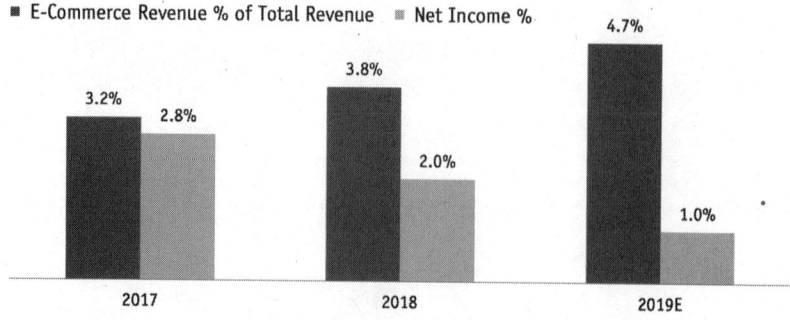

FIGURE 10 Walmart online growth relative to profitability. Source: "Wal-Mart Stores, Inc.: Revenues and Sales," eMarketer Retail, https://goo.gl/VqndAt.

A more effective strategy would have been to focus on current customers and get them to spend more. If Walmart had done that instead of trying to copy Amazon, and if their existing customers had spent one-third more in 2017, or 35% more than they actually did, the increase would have equaled Amazon's entire revenue and profit (see figure 11).

In 2017, Walmart's revenue was $500 billion and its net income was $9.8 billion. Amazon's revenue was $177 billion and its net was income $3 billion. Thus, if Walmart had grown its revenue and net income by 35%, its revenue would have increased by $175 billion and its net income by $3.4 billion—Amazon's total revenue and profit that year.

But instead of focusing on getting current customers to spend more, Walmart focused on getting new online customers to compete with Amazon—and they did this at the cost of profitability. Amazon, meanwhile, has continued to grow.

If you're wondering whether your company is becoming more like Walmart or more like Amazon, think about the following questions.

- How much more or less are your existing customers or customer segments spending now than they did a year ago? Two years ago?
- How have your margins changed?

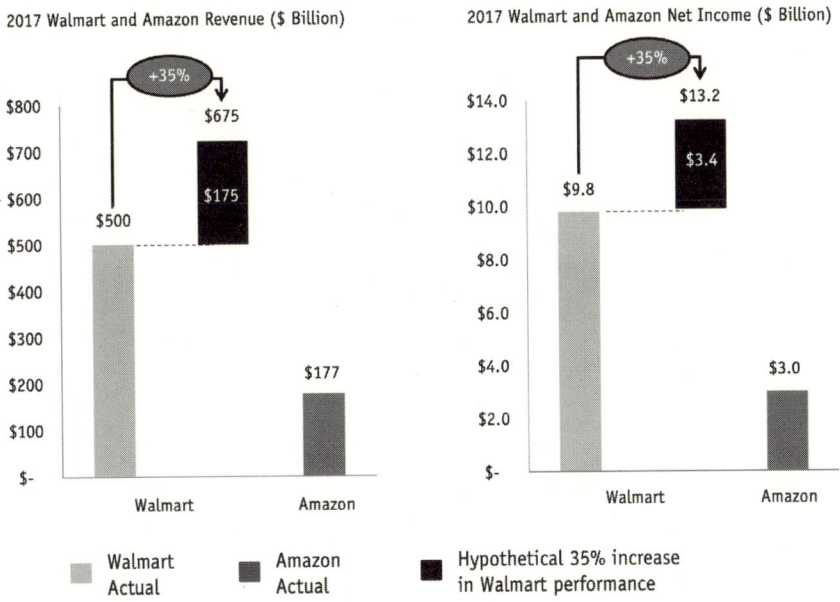

FIGURE 11 Walmart and Amazon actual and hypothetical revenues and profits. Sources: Walmart 2017 Annual Report, Wal-Mart Stores, Inc., March 31, 2017, https://goo.gl/dqxrpD; 2017 Amazon Annual Report, Amazon Investor Relations, February 1, 2018, https://goo.gl/bT84eT.

If neither customer spending nor margins are growing, you need to rethink your selling activities and focus on improving your business appeal to existing customers. The steps at the end of this chapter will show you how to do that.

GETTING CURRENT CUSTOMERS TO SPEND MORE

Study after study has shown that existing customers are likely to spend more and are more profitable than new customers. As the *Harvard Business Review* put it, "It makes sense: you don't have to spend time and resources going out and finding a new client—you just have to keep the one you have happy." Bain and Company found that "return customers tend to buy more from a company over time."[3] Yet, despite this, most companies cope with declining sales by chasing after new customers.

Take Whole Foods. Their customer base increased by 27% from 2013 to 2018, but their revenue per customer dropped, and so did their profit margins, even after Amazon acquired them.[4] The new customers simply did not spend as much as the old customers, and the margins on them were lower, too.

Even when businesses do focus on existing customers, most do it in old-fashioned ways that don't increase revenue.

Loyalty Programs Don't Work

Industries from airlines to supermarkets to rental cars have used loyalty programs for decades, promising customers that the more they spend, the more they'll get in discounts or other perks. U.S. marketers spend an estimated $90 billion on noncash loyalty programs, but that investment increasingly appears to be wasted. Accenture found that 54% of people said they'd switched providers in the past year, and 78% say they retract loyalty faster today than they did three years ago.[5] Retail, cable, bank, and home or business internet customers are most likely to switch.

But even though all this is well known, companies continue to shore up these loyalty programs. Macy's sales dropped, forcing store closures in 2015, yet, two years later, CEO Jeff Gennette said, "We are excited about our plans for the holiday, which is when Macy's truly shines as a gifting destination. The loyalty program, special in-store experiences, and a strong mobile and online presence will help drive holiday sales."[6] In 2017, Macy's reworked its Star Rewards loyalty program to add e-commerce perks like free shipping offers. Though Macy's did increase revenue by 1.3% during that holiday season, online retailers such as Wayfair and Amazon increased revenues on similar products much faster.

Companies with the highest brand loyalty do not have loyalty programs. As Dan Bane of Trader Joe's said, "We know that loyalty does not come from a special card or a so-called 'reward' you receive when you spend your hard-earned dollars in a store. At Trader Joe's, we would never test your loyalty by printing out a three-foot-long scroll of coupons for money off things the next time you shop in our stores. We reward your loyalty by pricing our products as low as they can go every single day. No coupons or club cards needed . . . ever."[7] While other grocery stores in the United States, such as Safeway and Supervalu, were closing stores, Trader Joe's was opening new ones.

Customers don't stick with a company because of its loyalty program. They stick with it because it meets their needs better than the competition does.

Customer Retention Programs Are Counterproductive

Other companies attempt to keep current customers by offering them incentives when they threaten to turn off service or cancel their accounts, by making it difficult for them to do it, and sometimes even by penalizing them for doing it. Punishing your customers with fines or forcing them to do something they don't want to do is bad for business.

Cable companies like Comcast are notorious for these tactics. In November 2014, a Comcast customer decided to disconnect his service, but for several hours the customer service representative refused to disconnect the service, citing one pretext or another. When this was publicly brought to the attention of Brian Roberts, Comcast CEO, he said, "I was embarrassed by a customer service debacle with a customer trying to disconnect his service." Then he promised to revamp the customer service department with new hires and new leadership. However, Comcast still encourages employees to force customers to buy services that they don't need and to make it almost impossible for them to cancel their service. Comcast's combative relationship with its customers continues, and it remains one of the most disliked companies in the United States.[8] Not surprisingly, its subscriptions keep shrinking.

"Customer retention program" now has negative connotations. To most people, it means forcing current customers to jump through hoops to negotiate a fair price. Though retention programs may bolster revenue in the short term, the long-term impact on customer relationships is devastating. Not surprisingly, cable companies, the worst offenders, are suffering from cord cutting at an unprecedented rate and are desperately merging with other, profitable companies to extend their lives.

Increased Service Levels Work but Need Thoughtful Execution

The third approach companies typically take in response to falling sales is to increase service, and that has shown better results. Businesses know that they will generate more revenue if they improve service levels. Customers consider some services—warranties, faster returns, and easy credit, for instance—as almost money-back guarantees. They also tend to love having a better selection of products, free shipping, help during shopping, and easy checkout, among other things. These all provide benefits to customers other than price. However, if companies aren't careful, the increased service levels can significantly reduce profit.

Take return policies. Most customers like lenient return policies; knowing they can easily return anything they don't like makes them buy with greater confidence. This is particularly true when they are buying online and have never touched the product. It's an insurance policy of sorts. Making returns easier for online purchases was what made e-commerce possible. However, returns cost retailers money. Post-Christmas returns typically cost retailers close to $300 billion, or 8% of purchases, every year. So now some retailers, including Amazon, are banning customers who return products too frequently.[9] This is understandable, but it could be counterproductive for sellers.

Let's look at what happened when Tumi tried it. Tumi's products—luggage, bags, backpacks, and the like—were known for their durability. Some had lifetime warranties. The luggage was expensive but it had a big fan following among frequent travelers because of its durability, lifetime warranty, and Tumi's no-questions-asked repair policy. In 2004, a private equity company bought Tumi, dropped prices to make the products attractive to more people, and decreased the famed lifetime warranty to five years. When Samsonite bought the line in 2016, they stopped honoring warranty commitments altogether. Now frequent flyers are recommending Briggs & Riley instead.[10] Lowering service levels is risky!

INCREASING SERVICE LEVELS WITHOUT RUINING YOURSELF

But increasing service levels is risky, too. When the financial services market started changing, one firm's high net worth customers asked for more support. Afraid of losing them, the firm added free personal bankers, investment specialists, 24/7 customer support, and other services. But the firm offered them to all customers and didn't charge any of them. Not surprisingly, this ate into the firm's profitability—so much so that they had to eliminate the popular new services. The trick, when it comes to increasing service levels, is to do it profitably. Otherwise, you will not be able to support the new service as it gains traction among your customers, and you may end up losing them when you make the inevitable cuts.

When companies give all their customers access to the same increased level of service, their costs may increase more than revenues, because a few customers end up overusing or abusing the new services levels. When customers don't have any incentives to choose an appropriate service level, some take advantage of the company's generosity. For example, they may return clothes even after wearing them—because they can. But there are ways around this for retailers. For example, instead of changing the return policy for everyone—even customers who never take advantage of it—retailers can ask abusers to pay return fees. Some may be willing to pay them.

Amazon has mastered the art of increasing service levels profitably. In 2005, Amazon wanted to increase its revenue and did it by identifying frequent buyers and asking them to pay for a new service: Prime. This was a financially risky move that completely changed the e-commerce industry. In those days, it took packages a week or longer to reach customers. Two-day shipping was an expensive luxury. But, as Bezos said when he started Prime, two-day shipping became "an everyday experience rather than an occasional indulgence."[11]

Amazon had almost 100 million Prime members as of 2018.[12] These customers are estimated to spend two to five times as much on Amazon as non-Prime members do. The fact that their shipping is "free" (many forget that they have actually already paid for it with their Prime fee) encourages them to buy more. Now, whenever Amazon offers new categories of products, Prime members automatically start buying them. Plus, customers who once would have gone to Walmart or Target when they needed something quickly now just buy it on Amazon, where prices were already lower.

With Prime, Amazon's shipping costs increased, but the membership fees more than made up for it. Amazon balanced the cost between high- and low-volume shippers and found alternate ways to generate revenue from their customer base. There was barely any pushback when Amazon increased its Prime annual fees from $79 to $99, in 2014.

Creating Service Levels That Competitors Find Difficult to Copy

The trouble with increasing service levels is that competitors can often copy you as soon as they see you winning customers. Eventually, the new service becomes the industry standard and increases costs for everyone as competitors try to provide similar services at a lower cost, or even for free, to attract customers. Walmart copied Prime's free two-day shipping, though Walmart had a minimum purchase requirement instead of a membership fee. Now Target and most other retailers have their own versions of two-day free shipping. For the holiday season of 2018, Target offered two-day free shipping without a minimum purchase requirement.[13]

The way to make money from your service levels is to make it difficult for the competition to copy you. Despite Walmart and Target introducing two-day free shipping, Amazon hasn't lost its Prime members. The reason is simple: Prime is bigger than two-day shipping. Over time, Amazon added Amazon video, music, photo storage, and many other services to Prime, which now has a 95% renewal rate.[14] As Amazon's chief financial officer admitted, Prime members who stream video renew their membership at "considerably higher rates" than those who don't, though these additional services have added costs for Amazon.

Amazon uses service levels well, and so do budget airlines. Traditional carriers like British Airways, Lufthansa, and others focus on business travelers, but budget airlines like Ryanair and easyJet concentrate on vacation travelers. Budget airline tickets in Europe can cost less than half the price of tickets from full-service carriers.

To do this profitably, budget airlines reduced their costs. They standardized their planes to get significant discounts from aircraft manufacturers, standardized operations, took advantage of fuel efficiency, removed unnecessary luxuries, turned around faster at gates to keep planes flying, and flew to cheaper airports. They made money by selling food on board and charging for amenities like extra luggage. Ryanair and Wizz made more money than Lufthansa, British Airways, and Air France.[15] When full-service airlines tried to copy the budget airlines model, Lufthansa with Eurowings and Air France with Transavia, they failed. Though the budget airline model was simple, it was tough to replicate. Budget airlines in Europe grew year over year by 7.1%, compared to 3.5% for full-service carriers, from 2007 to 2016.

Creating a service model that competitors find difficult to copy can create a sustainable competitive advantage. Amazon's revenue growth in the United States and the growth of budget airlines in Europe continues at a rapid pace, killing the big and mighty in their respective markets.

INCREASING REVENUE PROFITABLY

Walmart shows what a struggle it is to increase revenue profitably. Companies that do it successfully—like Amazon and the budget airlines—tailor their services to different customer segments and then convince customers to pay for those services. This compensates the companies for the increased cost of providing higher services. There are ways to segment customers in almost all industries.

Tumi, for example, could have offered its beloved lifetime warranty at an additional cost—there was no need to eliminate it completely. It could have kept its base price competitive *and* offered the warranty at an additional price. Instead, Tumi foolishly ended the warranty and lost its most loyal customers. And it never even asked them whether they would be willing to pay more for lifetime warranties!

Almost all companies can use the following step-by-step approach to increase service levels profitably.

- The first step is to identify customers by segment. Not all customers have the same needs, and segmenting allows you to understand what the important differences are.

- The second step is to identify the services that are valued by each of the segments. In the case of Tumi, the frequent travelers had different requirements than the casual travelers. Providing the right service to each segment is essential to ensuring they are valued.

- The third step is to create a range of services based on the different customer needs and to make them difficult for competitors to copy. Otherwise, the new service level will quickly become the industry standard and increase cost for everyone.

- The last step is to price the new service so that customers will be willing to pay for it.

The following example shows how we used these steps with a client, a leading wireless company. They needed help identifying gaps in their portfolio and developing a service model that would address them. They wanted to increase their revenue, but their customer demographic and psychographic segmentation did not show any opportunities for unique offerings.

Step 1: Identify Customer Segments

Most companies don't do customer segmentation well. They use methods that provide psychographic and demographic insights, which may be useful for marketing and advertising but is not useful for targeting of services, because these methods don't provide insights into buying behavior.

A better way is to segment the customer base by buying behavior that can be measured, such as usage or business metrics. This approach makes it easy to target customer segments with the service offerings valued by each.

But most companies use demographic segmentation. They segment customers by age, gender, race, and income. The assumption is that, somehow, everyone in each group will behave the same way and have the same needs. Anyone with two teenage daughters knows from experience how false this is! Some people in the same income group shop heavily online and some do not. There are early adopters of technology across all age groups, genders, and household income. Demographics are not a good way to identify people's willingness to buy products or services.

Other companies use psychographic segmentation and divide customers into segments based on their values, attitudes, lifestyles, and personalities. The wireless company, for example, segmented customers into psychographic groups such as empty nesters, professionals, or working single parents. You can spend hours discussing the profiles and characteristics of each one of these psychographic segments, but they won't help you predict unique service needs. A professional can be a heavy or a light wireless user. Those who travel frequently for work might use wireless data more than those who work in the office—but neither has anything to do with psychographics.

The third and least commonly used segmentation, called behavioral segmentation, is based on actual buying behavior, loyalty, usage, user status, and the like. Companies who use this method look at patterns of buying and using different products, then launch products of different sizes based on usage. For example, toothpaste is sold in different sizes in different countries according to usage patterns. Similarly, the design of loyalty programs is based on how frequently buyers purchase from a site or from stores.

Based on client work, I have found that the best way to segment customers is by business metrics such as volume/usage, profitability, or the strategic nature of the segment. For example, Amazon differentiates customers based on how much they shop online, irrespective of their lifestyle choices or demographics. A wireless company should understand the different needs of high- and low-usage customers.

For our wireless client, then, we created a survey to collect usage and purchasing behavior and other criteria from more than eight hundred respondents across the United States. For additional insight, we also used demographics to classify the respondents into four groups: mass market (people older than thirty years), youth (people younger than thirty years), business (companies with fewer than five hundred employees), and enterprise (companies with more than five hundred employees).

As we analyzed the data, it became clear that talk usage (minutes per month) provided more meaningful segmentation than the psychographic segmentation used by the company and the industry in general. There was a misperception that because people were on their phones all the time, everyone was using wireless services aggressively. In reality, phone usage meant far less; many people who were on their phones all the time were using Wi-Fi, because they were inside of buildings. A large number of customers were barely using wireless services, and the major wireless providers largely ignored their needs.

The heavy and light wireless (talk) users were very different. The high wireless users used more wireless data—sent more texts, used the web more, downloaded more content, and watched more videos. They valued better network connectivity over low prices. The low wireless users group used mainly voice, with some texting—only a small percentage used data. The low wireless user group was very price sensitive and switched providers frequently.

Figure 12 shows how low usage was in all segments. The low-usage group represented 22% of enterprise customers and 51% of mass market customers. On average, the low-usage group was close to 40% of the market. This group used mobile phones only when they were traveling outside the home or office. They cut across all traditional classifications, including business, youth, and mass market. From a demographics

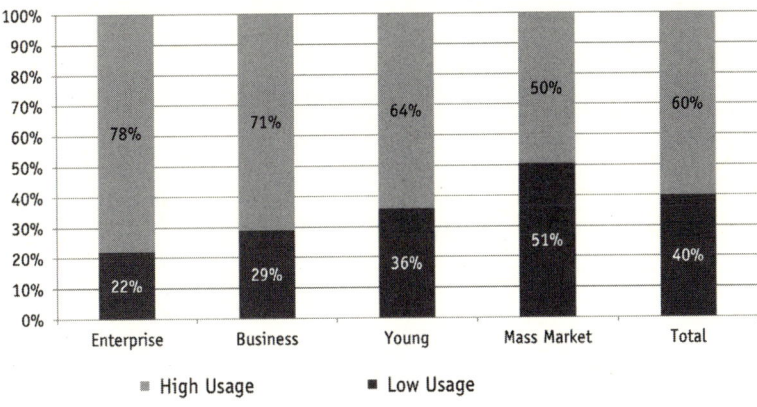

FIGURE 12 Low- and high-usage groups by classification. Source: Three S Consulting.

perspective, they were at all income levels, genders, races, and age groups. From an ethnicity perspective, though, the low-usage group was primarily white Caucasian as well as young Hispanic. The other ethnic groups were proportionately represented. Wireless companies consistently ignored this low-usage group and focused instead on capturing market share in the higher-usage segment by offering different data services. Yet, by doing this, they were potentially ignoring the needs of 40% of their customers, providing opportunities for low-cost entrants to disrupt the whole wireless market.

Step 2: Identify Services That Are Valued by Each Segment

Based on the segmentation study, we came up with four new segments to provide a more in-depth understanding of needs among the low-usage group (table 1). The exact need varied among the segments, but all of them were looking for one thing: low-cost calling and texting. They also all preferred to buy data packages, international calling, and roaming services based on specific, sometimes temporary needs—such as, for example, while traveling.

TABLE 1

Low-Usage Group Segments

ETHNICITY	CLASSIFICATION	NEED
White Caucasian	Mass market (older than thirty years)	Mostly part of a family plan Price-sensitive segment
White Caucasian	Young (younger than thirty years)	Prepaid services Willing to pay for affordable data services
White Caucasian	Business (fewer than five hundred employees)	Less price sensitive as business pays for wireless bills Willing to pay for affordable data services
Hispanic	Young (younger than thirty years)	Prepaid services Willing to pay for affordable international calling, roaming in Mexico, and affordable data services

Step 3: Create a Range of Services Based on Different Customer Needs

Creating a successful offering for the low-usage group required an entirely different approach than the traditional wireless model in the United States. Also, to be known for service, it was essential to develop a model that was difficult for the competition to match. Developing that kind of model is a competitive advantage when product differentiation is low, as it is for wireless service companies.

Our team studied the success of low-cost mobile models in other markets, which featured low base cost, no frills, and add-ons for which customers were willing to pay. We found that the prices had to be 30% lower than the cost of the full-service offering for it to be successful. To maintain a low cost, the company had to remove expenses wherever possible. Since handsets are a significant cost for users, we suggested that customers be allowed to use their existing handsets and not be required to sign contracts. We suggested low monthly prices with affordable add-on data plans, international calling, and roaming in Mexico.

The approach was similar to the one budget airlines use to attract cost-sensitive travelers. These airlines are successful because of their standardized planes, charges for frills, and faster operations. Budget airlines are the most profitable segment of the airline industry. We believed a budget mobile offering could become an equally profitable part of the wireless industry.

Step 4: Price the Service Appropriately So That Customers Will Be Willing to Pay for It

The critical challenge was to determine exactly how much each customer should be charged for service. This is hard to do, so companies typically use their own cost as a guide. Even then, companies lack a complete understanding of the cost of different services. A better way is to understand at what price point customers would get excited about the service, and then find a way to make it happen. It's the approach taken by Amazon. They launch a service, lose money, learn how to make it work, and then tweak it until customers start to adopt it.

That's the strategy we recommended to our wireless client. We warned them that it would lose money in the first few years, because of the high customer acquisition and network costs. As figure 13 shows, the client's major expenses were customer acquisition and network operations, which cost 36% and 33% of revenue, while other costs were relatively small. So we expected the company to lose about 5% of revenue during the new program's first few years.

To make the budget mobile offering financially viable, our plan focused on removing costs wherever possible. The plan made the offering available online, with no retail presence and no handset subsidy. The company contracted with multiple wireless providers to get preferential rates in different markets. Overhead work was outsourced. Automation was introduced to encourage automatic payments and to reduce customer support cost.

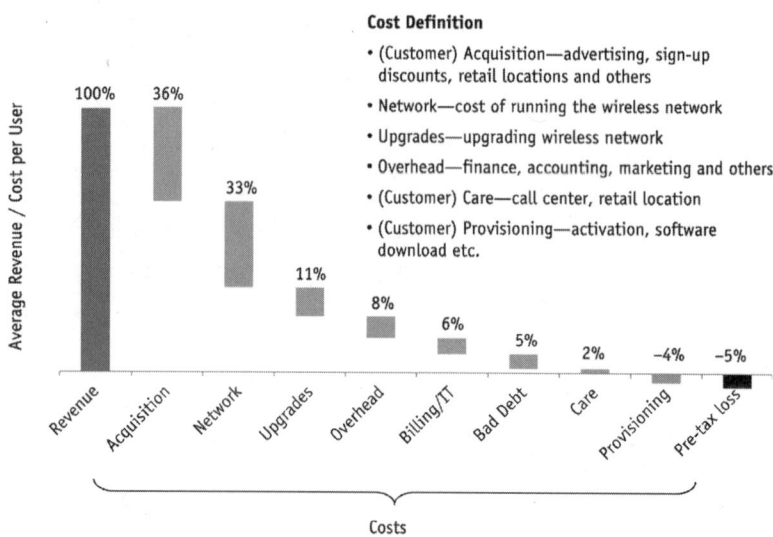

FIGURE 13 Estimated monthly revenue and cost per user. Source: Three S Consulting.

The profit, we hoped, would come from add-ons such as data plans, international calling, and roaming in Mexico. These were priced competitively and not at a discount. The assumption was that, as the company increased its subscriber base, it would be in a position to strike exclusive deals with wireless operators for the add-on services, thereby improving profitability substantially. The client launched a variant of the budget mobile offering as a prepaid service, and within a few years it was showing a profit.

Most Companies Can Profit from Following These Steps

A step-by-step approach like this can help companies to profitably increase revenue from their existing customer base. Even Amazon could learn from it. Though Amazon Prime has been wildly successful, not all of its customer segments are profitable. For instance, it's prohibitively expensive to send one or two shipments to rural homes. So Amazon is increasing its Prime membership cost again in 2018 to compensate. But by increasing membership costs, Amazon is gambling that its profitable customers will subsidize its loss-making routes. And now, Amazon has competition for its two-day shipping from Walmart, Target, and others. Eventually, customers will probably be put off by the price increases. Wouldn't it have been better for Amazon to develop a separate offering for rural or other unprofitable customers?

GETTING EXISTING CUSTOMERS TO SPEND MORE

Getting existing customers to spend more is the holy grail of business. Millions of customers continue to visit retail outlets, but they're spending less than they once did. That's the real reason for the failure of brick and mortar stores. It's not Amazon. Companies have to find new ways to meet their customers' needs so they'll spend more. But they have to do it in a way that increases profitability, too. Following the process laid out in this chapter will help them to grow revenue in a financially prudent way and have a higher chance of success.

Walmart, for example, could classify its stores by volume and profitability and then provide valet and home delivery at a reasonable price in high-volume stores. Walmart could potentially introduce other services, based on customer need. Would it improve customers' lives and would customers be willing to pay for the new services? They probably would, but we will never know unless Walmart offers them the services.

4

CUSTOMER-FOCUS STRATEGY 2: PERSONALIZATION IS NOT A LUXURY

PERSONALIZATION—MAKING PRODUCTS OR SERVICES that are tailored to each individual—is revolutionizing businesses. Personalization challenges all the fundamental concepts business leaders were taught from the day they started their career—concepts like "bigger is better" and "standardization." These concepts date from the Industrial Revolution, when companies didn't offer customers many choices but customers bought the mass-produced products anyway because they were so inexpensive.

That was then. Now, customers everywhere want personalized products and services, and they want them at affordable prices. Even companies beloved by their customers struggle with this. For example, although millennials love Starbucks and can't seem to resist a personalized cup of coffee with service, Starbucks's transactions haven't increased. That much is public knowledge, as are the company's repeated price increases. Starbucks's same-store sales growth has been steadily declining, as figure 14 shows. Same-store growth from transactions was reduced from 5% in 2013 to −1% in 2018, whereas value growth stayed between 2% and 4%. Thus, growth in the United States probably comes from current customers spending more, not more customers coming into the stores.[1]

The larger lesson here: personalization has to be affordable to attract customers. The younger generations, millennials in particular, want personalized products and services but won't pay premium prices for them. Thus, affordability is key for all companies now.

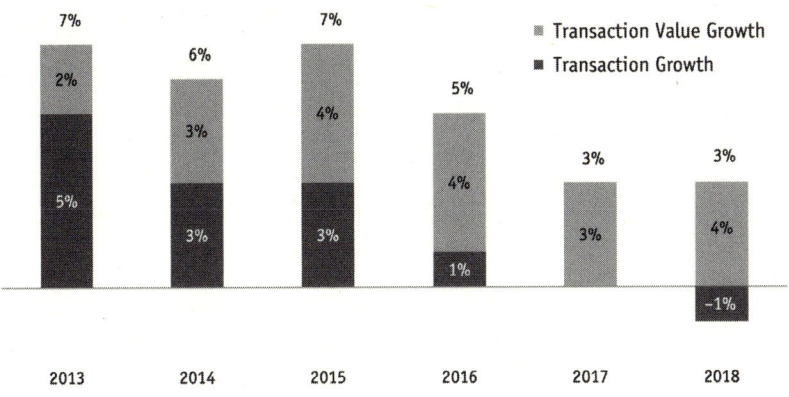

FIGURE 14 Starbucks same-store growth (percentage). Source: "Starbucks: Same-Store Sales," eMarketer Retail, https://goo.gl/DF3Zin.

Personalization is inherently expensive, but it can be made affordable by thinking outside the box about how to design, create, manufacture, and deliver products and services. A few companies are experimenting with personalization, but no one is doing it on a large scale. It's a big opportunity and a threat to all businesses.

The first to figure out how to produce affordable personalized products will gain huge competitive advantages. To make personalization affordable, leaders will have to think completely differently, create flexible operations, and reduce waste. Big factories producing large volumes won't work in the new personalization world. Production sizes will become smaller as products are custom-built for each customer. Companies will have to hire skilled labor to produce customized products instead of unskilled labor repeating tasks on production lines. Companies will have to rethink the supply chain and streamline it for different types of customer demands. And at the same time, they will have to find ways to avoid the waste that often comes with customization. Planning and optimizing operations to handle all this will take effort—and solutions will be unique to each company and its customers.

But affordability, being willing to start over completely, and being able to think outside the box are crucial for all companies venturing into personalization. If you're wondering whether you need to personalize, consider the following questions.

- How adept is your company at addressing customer needs rather than merely selling products or services?
- How personalized are your company's products or services?
- How affordable are your personalized offerings?

The degree to which you are doing any of these things is the degree to which your company is set up to sell to newer generations. Once millennials and Gen Z start dominating spending—and that will happen within the next five to ten years—everyone, like it or not, will be operating in a new world, with new rules, and personalization is one of them. Your company will either figure out how to personalize or it will wither away.

THE PERSONALIZATION REVOLUTION

Personalization is revolutionizing customer demand worldwide. Even Japan—once a bastion of luxury goods—has seen luxury companies' sales decline by 10% to 30%. In countries such as China, India, and others in the Asia-Pacific region, local brands are winning over international brands. Customers in developing markets are looking for products that are tailored to their needs and not to the needs of those in the West. Look at Amazon's struggle in China. Their 2016 market share was 1.3% of all online retail—down from 2.1% in 2011—while Chinese e-commerce giants Alibaba and JD.com continue to hold a sizable market share (see figure 15).[2]

So why is the company credited with changing the U.S. retail landscape barely making a dent in China? It's not nationalism, which is the explanation most Western executives give. It's that Amazon's global offering does not attract Chinese customers. Memberships of any kind,

2016 Market Share—Online Retailers   Amazon's Market Share in China

FIGURE 15 Amazon's share of China online market. Source: Euromonitor, embedded figure, in Liza Lin and Laura Stevens, "Why Amazon Isn't Ready for Prime Time in China," *Wall Street Journal*, August 27, 2017, https://goo.gl/DKnQHk.

even those providing free shipping, aren't popular in China. This is true of all generations in China.

Worldwide, millennials are rejecting the concept of buy, buy, buy—and some boomers are becoming converts as they retire or downsize. Millennials don't want to pay twenty dollars for movie tickets or hundreds or thousands of dollars on fixing big houses or playing golf at country clubs.[3] Many don't want cars, if they can manage without them (they'd rather live where they can walk or ride-share), or expensive jewelry. They embrace simple living or minimalism, and some of their values are rubbing off on boomers. Some retirees are downscaling to tiny houses. Born out of frustration at too much clutter and growing debt, more and more people in all generations have become aware of how our consumption affects not only our wallets but also our planet. Many are rejecting paper napkins, plastic straws, and even clothes that clutter our landfills. This has resulted in some companies, including Burberry and H&M, burning tons of unsold clothes.[4]

But although the new generations of shoppers—millennials and Gen Z—are conscious of waste, averse to risk, and less likely to spend money unnecessarily, they do spend money. And they will pay for personalized services they love. Some will pay to have gourmet meals delivered, or even for their own (temporary) butlers or personal chefs.

Companies struggling to remain relevant and profitable can use this trend to breathe new life into their customer connections by offering affordable personalized services. Charging premium prices for "customization"—or, worse, trying to make money off of premium services—won't work. Coming up with ways to deliver affordable personalization to the masses will, and that will generate far more revenue and profit than premium services for just a select few.

Personalization is becoming increasingly in demand worldwide, and making it affordable is the way forward.

Early Attempts at Personalization

The trend toward personalization started with websites. As customers searching sites grew frustrated at all the irrelevant information, tech companies figured out how to show only relevant content. E-commerce sites took that a step further by recommending new items based on previous purchases—though many early attempts were (and still are) clumsy and annoying. No one likes to be shown a new laptop just after buying one!

Sephora, a cosmetics store, found a novel way to use customer data. They began recommending products based on the shopper's skin tone. In the past, women often found cosmetics that matched their coloring by trial and error. Sephora alone had 110 shades, and finding the right one took a lot of effort and time on the part of the salesperson and customer. But Sephora customers could create profiles, and with those, Sephora could quickly and easily match products to each shopper. Customers loved the personalized recommendations. While the rest of the retail cosmetics industry declines, Sephora continues to grow.

Other companies are figuring out how to recommend clothes, furniture, and many other items. For example, Stitch Fix and Nordstrom Trunk provide online personal assistant services that could recommend clothes and send a box of them based on customer preference and style. All the customer has to do is complete an interactive questionnaire comparing different styles, and with that, the company learns what the customer likes.

Other ways in which companies are personalizing products include more fun packaging and labeling. To celebrate its fiftieth anniversary in the United Kingdom, Heinz (whose beans are very popular there) gave customers the option of putting their names on the beans can. Similarly, sneaker companies such as Nike and Adidas are providing limited customization by allowing customers to choose shoes' color, type, and logo size.

However, these efforts are nowhere near the personalization the new generations want. Recommending existing products or services based on customer data and personalization are not personalization. Personalization means creating unique products or solutions based on an individual's wishes. True personalization wouldn't be choosing your sneaker color; it would be sneakers made just for you. The sneakers would be shaped precisely for your foot measurements, arch height, and even how you walk or run. So we are a long way from real personalization.

Personalizing Luxury Goods Now

Luxury companies that have successfully weathered many market changes—and even those that offer personalization to a select few—are having a difficult time surviving in the new era. The industry is in a steady decline due to a long, steady decline in new customer growth. Millennials don't spend on luxury. Fundamentally, luxury brands' use of exclusivity as an enticement doesn't resonate with millennials, Gen Z, and some boomers. Instead, these customers prefer more personalized, affordable luxuries. Uber and Airbnb are the new luxury players.

They are making luxuries like chauffeur-driven cars and apartments or cottages in desirable locations available to millennials at affordable prices and on demand.

Traditional luxury companies are having a difficult time adjusting. For some time, growth in the luxury business has come from price increases, not volume. Now, when even the rich are reluctant to pay exorbitant prices, luxury goods companies need to reach out to millennials. But they don't do this well. They shun online sales, and their old ways of advertising don't resonate with millennials, either. Millennials think of status symbols as excesses of the rich.[5] Celebrity endorsements for luxuries don't fly with millennials.

Consider Tiffany. They had a brutal 2016 holiday sales season, and a host of executives, including the CEO, left the company. The trend toward declining sales started in mid-2014 and continued into 2017. Tiffany's U.S. yearly growth declined from 6% in 2014 to 2% in 2017, while total U.S. luxury market sales declined from 8% to –1% (see figure 16).

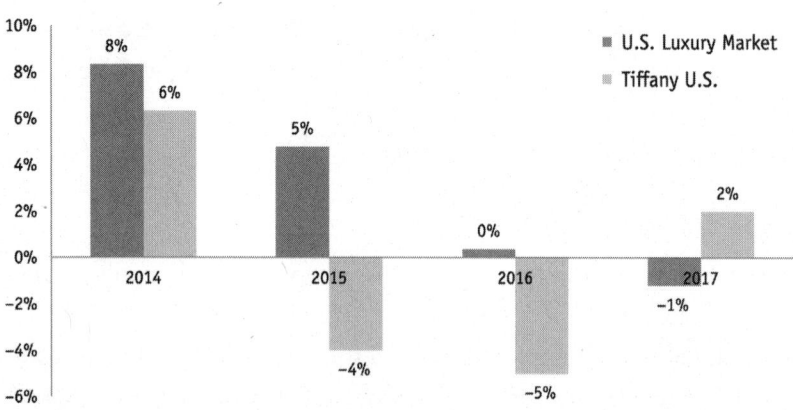

FIGURE 16 Year-over-year growth of luxury sales, Tiffany's and U.S. market. Sources: "Market Value of Luxury Goods in the United States from 2013 to 2018 (in Million U.S. Dollars)," Statistica, https://goo.gl/xoeAWQ; "Tiffany & Co.: Revenues and Sales—Americas," eMarketer Retail, https://goo.gl/6rf4YL.

Tiffany & Co. is not alone. Other luxury companies are facing troubles as well. Neiman Marcus, Saks Fifth Avenue, and Nordstrom are dealing with a continued sales decline in all markets except China. Even the largest luxury brand, LVMH (Louis Vuitton Moët Hennessy), is cautious about growth prospects.

Disrupters are providing the quality, style, artistry, and design that are associated with luxury goods, at an affordable price point. Luxury goods companies will have a better chance of success if they embrace affordable personalization.

PERSONALIZATION THEN AND NOW

Complexity and costs are the biggest challenges companies face when trying to provide personalization. Before the industrial revolution, all products were personalized. If you needed something, you either made it yourself or you hired someone to make it for you. The cost of many things was so high that only the rich could afford them. In the Middle Ages, for example, a nobleman's goblet or a lady's dress could cost as much as a middle-class person's farm. Most people owned very little.

Then companies began standardizing and mass producing products so that more people could buy them, as Henry Ford did when he made a car for the masses. But there was no choice; as he said, buyers could have their cars painted any color, "as long as it's black." There was a trade-off: no choices, but you could actually own a car. There was no option to pay a little more to have red instead of black or four doors instead of two. The production processes didn't allow for variation. They were designed according to the principles of economy of scale and "bigger is better."

This is basically how many products are still manufactured, though, over time, companies started providing the customer with some choices. You can now get cars in different sizes and colors, but only the very, very rich can have a car made just for them. You have to pick what's available in the market. Companies still try to lower costs with bigger factories. Globalization has centralized production even more, with large factories catering to customers all around the world. Think of Apple's megafactories in China that employ 450,000 people doing repetitive work.

At factories like this, personalization is a disaster waiting to happen. Big factories are geared toward high-volume production, and modifying a single item is difficult. Increased cost and complexity continue beyond production, to managing the new personalized products, marketing them, storing them, and getting them to customers. And besides all this, someone has to customize what is being made for each customer. If you get your clothes tailored, you know that fitting your clothes can cost as much as the clothes themselves. Why? You have to hire a tailor locally, and their time costs more than that of the people making the clothes in other countries.

More and more research is showing that, even without personalization, the linkage between volume and profit is diminishing. In some industries, such as the automobile industry, volume is actually an impediment to increasing profit. This is because companies have to produce in such large volumes to keep their factories running that, as customer demand shifts, they either discount the products or write off their production costs. Only five automakers worldwide—Subaru, Great Wall (China), Maruti Suzuki (India), BMW, and Daimler/Mercedes—made money beyond the cost of capital (which is the minimum return expected by investors) during the 2012 to 2017 period.[6] As table 2 shows, the companies making money are small to midsize. Big is no longer better in the auto industry!

Subaru is able to deliver returns above the cost of capital because it makes different cars for different customer segments, and does so skillfully. Subaru first focused on customers seeking good off-road vehicles, then expanded its offerings to other segments.[7] This strategy brings the company loyal customers who are willing to pay full price—Subaru rarely discounts its cars. So although Subaru is a small company with only one quarter the revenue of Toyota, its profit margin is close to double Toyota's.

TABLE 2

Size and Profitability of the Auto Industry

COMPANY SIZE	LOSS	RETURN BELOW COST OF CAPITAL	RETURN ABOVE COST OF CAPITAL
Large (more than 4 million vehicles per year)		Volkswagen Toyota General Motors Renault-Nissan Hyundai-Kia Ford SAIC Fiat Chrysler	
Medium (2 million to 4 million vehicles per year)	Peugeot Chongqing Changan	Honda Dongfeng Motor Suzuki BAIC	Daimler BMW
Small (less than 2 million vehicles per year)	GAC Tesla	Mazda Tata Motors Mitsubishi	Maruti Suzuki Great Wall Subaru

NOTE: Returns estimates based on 2012–2017 averages of annual WACC/ROIC ratios. Source: Gadfly Calculations, embedded figure, in David Fickling, "Size Isn't Everything, Big Auto," *Bloomberg*, August 1, 2017, https://goo.gl/vZqnFG.

Subaru's small size works well for it. Yasuyuki Yoshinaga, the Subaru CEO, said in May 2017, "We only make a million cars. I have absolutely no intention to make that two million."[8] The fact that Subaru has stayed small and stayed profitable is one more example of how the old bigger is better strategy no longer works, though the rest of the auto industry still seems to think it does.

The concept of scale is getting questioned in other industries, too— in consumer goods, high tech, and many others—as smaller companies have started to beat larger companies with niche products that better address customers' needs. And this trend will only increase as more and more companies begin to personalize their offerings.

HOW TO DELIVER AFFORDABLE PERSONALIZATION

Whoever figures out how to make personalization affordable will be the next Amazon. Someone will. It is possible, if you do three things.

- First, rethink your offerings. Instead of thinking of them as products and services, think of them as solutions addressing customer needs, for which customers will pay.
- Then overhaul your operations by moving to distributed manufacturing and involving local suppliers.
- Finally, reduce waste.

Companies can only do all of this if they think outside the box and challenge their traditional ways of doing business. There is no one way to do it that will work for all companies. Each company and industry has unique challenges to overcome and advantages to leverage. What is common to all of them, when implementing personalization affordably, is a willingness to start over. Leaders who are prepared to let go of their old assumptions, traditions, and previously successful methodologies and open their minds to new ones are best positioned for reinvention and growth.

Step 1: Rethink Offerings

Most industries think of their offerings as something tangible—products and services. So they create a range of products and try to fit customer needs to them. Look at the apparel industry and its brands. They all produce trousers, shirts, suits, and other garments in a few sizes and fits. You can buy the same shirt at Ralph Lauren, Calvin Klein, Hugo Boss, Michael Kors, Banana Republic, and other stores, with a little variation in fabric or cut. Most will sell you the shirt based on your collar size and body structure (fit). You can expect to pay anywhere from $20 to

$200, depending on the brand you choose. Though these companies like you to believe it's their brand that makes you look better, actually it's the fabric and how the garment fits your body. That's why tailoring is coming back in vogue.

What if companies took a different approach and sold individually tailored clothes (offering a selection of fabric and fitting) to each customer? People will love these clothes because they'll look better in them—and even when they buy them online, the clothes will fit. What we are talking about here goes way beyond what the garment industry now offers, such as suits tailor-made for you. In New York City, that will cost you a few thousand or more, depending on fabric and timing. During the holidays, tailors are busy, and you pay more. After New Year's, prices drop. Those who don't want to pay for a custom-made suit can buy one and then have it altered. It will not fit as well as one made for you, but the alterations will cost less.

What doesn't exist now is an affordable fully tailored suit. Tailors in large metropolitan cities are expensive—not just because of their own cost of living and expenses but because of low volumes. In the past, companies in Hong Kong tailored suits for U.S. customers at affordable prices, through the mail. However, the younger generations in Hong Kong preferred other professions, so tailors were in short supply and prices went up.[9]

Now, a company called A Suit That Fits is bringing back the concept of bespoke (made to order) suits at an affordable price. You visit a local style advisor, who helps you choose the fabric. They measure you, make the suit in a developing country like India, and then do the final fitting locally. You only have to wait a few weeks—less than you normally wait for a New York tailor to make you a suit. And you will end up paying a quarter of the cost of a bespoke suit made in the United States, and about half what you'd pay for a good suit you had altered.

Why does it cost so much less? The company buys fabric in bulk, uses inexpensive labor, and doesn't waste any finished products. A lot of factory-made clothes never sell and end up in landfills if they don't sell after deep discounts. This has a considerable cost. With bespoke suits, there is no waste of the finished products, and the companies can pass these savings on to customers. Not surprisingly, A Suit That Fits is getting rave reviews. The company already has thirty-four studios across the United Kingdom, Ireland, and the United States, and is growing quickly.

Similar approaches could work for much of the garment industry if customers were willing to pay just a little more and companies were willing to think outside of the box. Some companies are already starting. J. Hilburn provides custom-made shirts, trousers, and accessories. Their products are of higher quality and last longer than most. A typical office shirt costs between $100 and $200, and dress pants range from $200 to $600, with a limited selection of fabric. The mass appeal at this price point is likely limited. However, if the company could reduce the cost by 50% or more, it could completely change the apparel industry.

Mtailor, on the other hand, takes your measurements with an app and provides custom-fit clothes at a more reasonable price. They claim that their measurements are 20% better than those of professional tailors. But you don't get to select the fabric before buying. You have to rely on the company to make the right choice for you.

Companies could offer custom tailoring in a variety of ways—customers could go to a local style advisor, who would measure them (for a fee) or do the measuring themselves, with their smartphones. The company could let customers choose the fabric, then send everything to be made either closer to where the customer lives or offshore. Customers also could be offered flexibility when it comes to delivery; the clothes made close to them might cost more but arrive sooner. Or customers could choose to pay a fixed delivery fee per year, like Amazon Prime customers. Final fittings (if needed) could be done locally, again for a fee. The company could store your measurements and offer seasonal promotions.

Personalization can work affordably in other industries, too. Ride-hailing companies are already offering it, using underemployment and unused cars as resources to provide personalized services. The drivers aren't making enough money to buy cars, so Uber and others are aggressively pushing for autonomous vehicles to replace their drivers. The user benefits of autonomous vehicles over ride-hailing services is unclear. The assumption is that it will reduce customers' costs, but the cars' prices may make the rides just as expensive for customers as hiring a driver. These autonomous cars may be workable only in high-traffic areas such as large cities. In low-traffic suburban areas, autonomous cars could mean higher costs for companies and customers or longer wait times for rides. It's too soon to tell whether any of these will appeal to people more than current and emerging solutions, such as Via, do.

But what if car companies thought outside the box? Commuters spend a lot of time stuck in traffic. What if a flying taxi took you to work? Drones with electric engines (lighter than gasoline engines) and autonomous flying may make this affordable. As we discussed in chapter 1, Boeing, Airbus, and a host of companies are experimenting with the flying taxi concept. Would you be willing to pay a little more for a faster commute, one that allowed you to live in a less expensive suburb that didn't work for you when your commute time was longer? More customers might love this kind of economic trade-off and time-saving option.

To make personalization happen, companies will have to change their points of view. They'll have to think about what to offer and how to deliver it by starting with their customers' needs, not with their own products. For example, most car companies presently think of themselves as manufacturers of vehicles. If they changed their point of view to start thinking of themselves as providers of transportation services, they'd be more likely to see personalized solutions that appeal to customers.

The same kind of change in thinking is needed in any industry, to make personalization happen. For example, most pharmaceutical companies think of themselves as companies producing medicines. If they thought of themselves as companies that improve their customers' quality of life and health, they'd succeed better with personalization.

Step 2: Create Flexible Operations

For personalization to work, companies will need operations that can create and deliver individual products in a cost-effective manner. Operations have to become flexible. How this will happen, of course, depends upon the company, but these are some of the ways to make operations flexible enough for affordable personalization.

Rethink manufacturing, from centralized to distributed. The most significant barrier to personalization is how companies think about operations. Most manufacturing sites are designed to produce large volumes with few variations. They employ unskilled labor to do simple jobs and depend on substantial capital investment. They trade flexibility for quantity and low per-unit manufacturing cost.

This trade-off doesn't work with personalization. To personalize, you need more flexible manufacturing that can create many variations. Companies will have to reduce output to increase variations.

You can see how this could affect the apparel industry. Huge clothing factories producing large volumes with unskilled labor can't personalize their clothes. Doing that takes tailors who can cut and make clothes for each order differently. So, to personalize, companies will have to hire more skilled workers. They'll also need to specialize in optimizing processes. Some in the garment industry might produce only men's suits (which require heavier materials and different cutting tools), while others concentrate on shirts. In other words, you need an entirely new way of thinking about production: distributed manufacturing.

In a distributed manufacturing environment, smaller production sites cater to demands quickly and creatively. The sites are flexible and specialized enough to produce personalized products, which for most companies means hiring and training more skilled labor. Companies can achieve both expertise and savings by using local vendors and talent. Local vendors and talent will bring a host of knowledge about unique local conditions—and possible savings in areas like buying supplies or getting things fixed.

In some industries, new technologies may provide opportunities and possibilities for personalization. For example, 3-D printing is changing how companies make prosthetic arms. You could consider 3-D printing as a form of distributed manufacturing. Instead of buying arms from a medical devices company, hospitals or doctor's offices print them locally for their patients. In other industries, programmable machines and robots could provide personalized products and services.

The challenge will be to make these affordable for mass adoption. And no one should overly rely on technology; it may be cheaper to use labor. That's plentiful throughout the world and variable in cost, unlike technology. But we're still at the beginning of the personalization revolution. The choices may not be that stark, and robots or other things we can't even imagine today may become affordable aids to humans in the future.

Create different supply chains for different demand. Personalization requires flexible supply chains, too. Most companies have a single supply chain that caters to all customers. This—like all one-size-fits-all approaches—impedes growth. The supply chain gets bogged down by complexity. To achieve flexibility, companies must create supply chains that cater to different demand patterns differently. They need suppliers that specialize in specific areas. For example, suppliers of synthetic clothes may be different from suppliers for cotton clothes. Only by analyzing the customer demand can companies figure out how to best configure their supply base to support their personalized offering.

The critical question is where to separate the supply chain by demand patterns. Do you separate them at supplier, in manufacturing, or at distribution centers? It mostly depends on where the customization is happening. In the case of the apparel industry, if the customization is happening at the manufacturing site, then the supply chains should be separated at manufacturing. However, if fabrics are customized, then the supply chain should be separated from the supplier end. Managing separate supply chains increases cost and effort, so design should be done carefully.

Reduce lead time. The second biggest customer complaint about personalized products is that they take too long to arrive. Though customers love personalized products, they will not wait long for them. Improving supply chain network design, changing the focus of supplier relationships from costs to flexibility, simplifying transaction processing, and improving information connectivity with partners all have been shown to reduce time to market.

In many companies, supply chain designs are rarely reviewed periodically. That won't work with personalization. Supply chain designs must be evaluated every few years to optimally service changes in demand. And companies should be prepared for this to entail opening or closing manufacturing sites or warehouses.

Suppliers play a critical role in getting products to market in a timely fashion. Most supplier contracts now focus far too heavily on cost and don't require flexibility. Contracts need to include the capacity to accommodate peak demand, scaling for new products, the ability to switch products quickly, and many other stipulations. Similar conditions also should be specified with logistics providers, contract manufacturers, and any other partners that help the company deliver its products or services to customers.

Transaction processing involves cutting purchase orders, approving invoices, and paying suppliers, among other things. In many companies, processing transactions has become highly bureaucratic, with multiple approvals required to reduce risk. In some cases, getting a purchase order takes as long as getting a supplier to deliver products! To respond quickly, companies must simplify the process—and they must do that without compromising on risk. Technology can help. Catalogs with agreed pricing and algorithms to flag exceptions can streamline transaction processing significantly.

Sharing information with suppliers continues to be a challenge in many industries. Companies have invested heavily in enterprise resource planning systems to get up-to-date information about demand and supply. Unfortunately, many still use e-mails to share order and other transaction information with their suppliers. This not only introduces error but also significantly increases lag time, since someone has to code the e-mailed information into the software. A better approach would be to link the information systems with suppliers, with adequate network protection against hacking. Many companies reply to this suggestion with the excuse that connecting with the supplier systems is too expensive. However, this doesn't wash. The cost of connecting with supplier systems has gone down significantly in recent years—and the benefits far outweigh the costs.

Step 3: Reduce Raw Material Waste

Waste of raw material is a real concern in a personalized product world because every order is different and has to be made to customer specification. In some industries, a significant amount of material could be wasted. In the apparel industry, for example, cutting out one garment from a few yards of fabric instead of using the same fabric for thousands of garments and using almost every scrap—could waste fabric. So it's essential that operations be designed efficiently to reduce waste throughout the process. For example, to minimize waste, computer programs could be created that would optimize fabric utilization based on current and anticipated demand. Without this kind of planning, personalized products can't be affordable. Optimization of operations will become one source of competitive advantage.

Affordability is vital to personalization. Companies that achieve it sustainably will dominate their markets.

MAKING AFFORDABLE PERSONALIZATION A REALITY

Personalization is a 180-degree change for most corporations. They are all tuned for mass production and would rather sit out the personalization fad. But new generations have made the fad a permanent reality. You either choose to play or go home.

With Sephora and others, we see very initial efforts at personalization. They are matching personal customer information with products that fit customer preference. Vistaprint and Shutterfly are making personalized photo albums, enabling users to design their own photo albums with a variety of layouts, fonts, and colors. Squarespace is doing the same for websites, offering hundreds of different templates for customized looks. Services like these cost a fraction of what a graphic designer would charge. More and more retailers are providing personal stylist services, if users are willing to share their personal preferences. However, we are still a long way from real personalization.

The challenges with personalization stem primarily from the costs associated with providing these services. To make personalization a reality, companies will have to think differently. They have to think from a customer's perspective instead of beginning from their products and services. Affordability is key—and the benefits to both companies and their customers could literally be life-changing.

Consider health care. Today, only the rich in the United States receive home visits and 24/7 access to their own personal doctor. Everyone else has to visit a hospital or doctor's office—and usually wait. But what if you could have a video visit with a doctor in India or in another country, where health care costs less than it does in the United States? The cost—in both time and money—of answers to non-emergency medical questions could become significantly cheaper. You'd still have to visit a lab for blood work, but the rest could be monitored from a distant location through your smartphone. Only in an emergency would you need to go to a hospital. Health care could become personalized and affordable—if only we think outside the box instead of optimizing an old model.

The stakes may not be as high in other industries—for customers—but the rewards for outside-the-box thinking can be just as high for companies. And in any industry, companies that don't offer their customers personalized products and services at affordable prices will lose out to companies that do. As millennials and Gen Z become the dominant buying group, the demand for personalized services will increase significantly.

This is both an opportunity and a threat. It's a threat because none of today's dominant companies have invested significantly in personalization and are still running on old paradigms. But it's an opportunity because no one knows who the winners will be. Whoever they are—upstarts or established companies thinking outside the box and unafraid to start over—they will be the next Apples or Amazons, companies that will dominate for a long time. Personalized services are sticky; once customers find a company that gives them exactly what they want, personalized just for them, they keep coming back.

5

CUSTOMER-FOCUS STRATEGY 3: CUSTOMERS WON'T WAIT

W E LIVE IN AN era of instant gratification. Whether they're buying a car or a custom-made suit, customers want it their way, now. And if you can't deliver it fast enough, they'll buy it from someone who can. Online, waiting even a few seconds is too much for some customers.[1] When sites load too slowly, they abandon their shopping carts and go straight to the competition—and with the range and ready availability of competing products in almost any field, there's plenty of it. But leaders still believe brand loyalty will somehow make their customers willing to wait while they develop or deliver products. Those days are long gone.

Consider Under Armour. The company created synthetic fibers to keep athletes dry and cool, even during heavy workouts—and the clothes caught on. Soon, people who didn't even play sports were buying them, and even Nike and Adidas couldn't compete with the upstart company. Then the company's customers wanted workout clothes that performed like Under Armour's offerings but were fashionable, too. But the company kept its focus on clothes for athletes. It offered Curry sneakers—great for basketball, but not fashionable. No one wanted them. Unable to adjust to their changing market, Under Armour's revenue and profitability plummeted. From 2011 to 2017, its revenue growth declined from 39% to 3%, while net income declined from 7% to −1% (figure 17).

Under Armour is not the only company to ignore its customers' needs! Many companies stick to what's worked for them in the past.

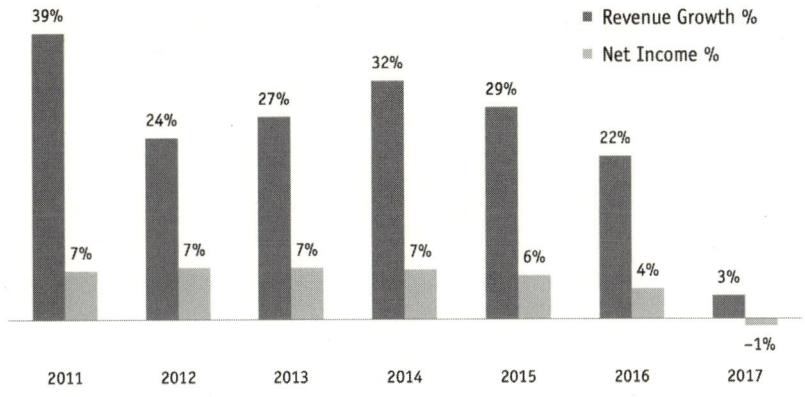

FIGURE 17 Under Armour's year-over-year revenue growth and net income. Source: "Financials," Under Armour, https://goo.gl/qGJaFf.

Some sit out a change, claiming it's a fad. Others have invested so much in their products or services that they're afraid to let them go. Still others think they can't justify the cost of developing new products.

Look at what used to be one of America's most successful companies. In 2012, Coca-Cola dominated markets worldwide. But then people decided they wanted healthier drinks. New York City Mayor Michael Bloomberg even tried to prohibit the sale of oversize sweetened drinks and to make sizes over sixteen ounces illegal, hoping to lower obesity rates. Coke and others sued, and they won the legal battle. But they lost the war. The court battle revealed how the industry had suppressed news on links between sugar and obesity, and that made healthier drinks even more popular than they already were.

In 2016, per capita Coke consumption dropped to a thirty-one-year low—and competitors like Indra Nooyi, the PepsiCo CEO, started investing in healthier drinks and snacks. From 2012 to 2017, Coca-Cola's revenue declined from 3% to −15% and PepsiCo's revenue increased from −2% to 1%. Also, Coca-Cola's net income declined from 19% to 3% while PepsiCo's declined only marginally, from 9% to 8% (figure 18).

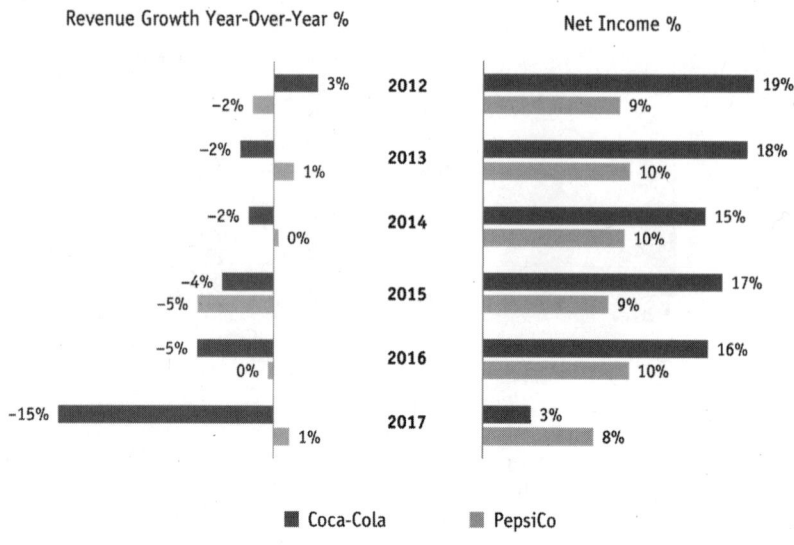

Revenue Growth Year-Over-Year %   Net Income %

FIGURE 18 Coca-Cola and PepsiCo year-over-year revenue growth and net income. Sources: "Annual and Other Reports," Coca-Cola Company, https://goo.gl/RZeVrB; "Annual Reports and Proxy Information," PepsiCo, https://goo.gl/QgWCFx.

Successful companies embrace change, challenging as it often is. They spot new needs and respond with new offerings before the competition does—and then change again before competitors can respond. Consider Amazon's approach to reading. Although Amazon sold more paper books than anyone, when they realized that customers wanted e-books, they brought out the Kindle, long before their competitors had a similar product. Then, when audiobooks became popular, Amazon made them available too—for a fee. Amazon stays popular because, when customers' needs change, Amazon offers new products before anyone else does, at cost-effective prices.

But most companies don't respond that well to changing customer needs, even companies that have been very successful with their old products. They don't plan. They make customers wait and lose their hard-earned success to competitors. Consider Tesla. Its first electric car was hugely popular and outperformed other high-end cars. But when the company tried to develop a mass-market car, it stumbled. In fact, the company went through what Musk called "production hell."

At first, all went well. Customers were enthusiastic at the prospect of buying a Tesla for $35,000, and the company eagerly took orders for five hundred thousand cars and offered refundable deposits. But Tesla had no experience with mass production, and the learning curve was steep. It was rumored that some of the parts in the Model 3 were hand-made. There were reported labor issues due to mass firings related to union issues and challenges with Tesla's ramp-up in China.[2] Tesla could barely produce five thousand vehicles a week by the middle of 2018! It never met its delivery dates and had to return the deposits.

How could they get this so wrong? Their first products were for early adopters, who were buying a Tesla as a second car. These customers were willing to wait. But mass-market customers, counting on their new car, were not. While Tesla missed deliveries and returned deposits, and China was making plans to ban gas- and diesel-powered cars, competitors got their electric cars ready. Tesla created the need for electric vehicles, but competitors like General Motors (GM) and BMW were the ones who benefited, while Tesla was battling short sellers and negative news from Musk's antics.

Having a winning product or being first in a field, like Tesla, is no good unless you embrace change. When customers' needs change, successful companies come up with new products or services, speed up their design and production, and deliver the new products quickly, at affordable costs. If you don't, your competitors will.

Thinking about these questions will help you assess how competitive your company is.

- How quickly does your company notice and respond to changing customer needs?
- How long does your company take to develop new products, bring them to market, and create effective service models?
- How quickly are other companies in your industry doing these things?

Your answers are a good guide to how long your company will remain successful. And if you are a new entrant, answering these questions about dominant players will help you identify opportunities for disruption.

INTRODUCE NEW PRODUCTS OR SERVICES QUICKLY

Companies spend an inordinate amount of time designing their products or services. Most have a complicated process for developing and testing new ideas, to avoid failure and financial risk. Unfortunately, the steps are often so cumbersome that many a good idea gets squelched. And the whole cycle of testing can take so long that by the time the product actually launches, customer needs have changed or more nimble competitors have captured the market.

The mobile payment market in China provides a case in point. Alipay was formed to deal with the lack of trust between Chinese buyers and sellers. Each side always suspected the other of fraud, and this lack of trust impacted e-commerce volume. So, in 2004, Alibaba, the huge Chinese e-commerce giant, launched Alipay. The service kept the buyer's payment in escrow and did not release it to the seller until the buyer had confirmed receipt of the product. Alipay resolved the trust issues and Alibaba's volume increased significantly. By 2013, Alipay had 80% of China's mobile payment market. But then customers wanted something different: a direct, peer-to-peer payment service. Alibaba did nothing.

In 2014, WeChat, which had started as the Chinese equivalent of WhatsApp (the cross-platform messaging and VoIP service owned by Facebook), came out with an innovative idea that was easy to sell to Chinese customers. WeChat took advantage of an old Chinese custom, *hongbao*. Hongbao are the red envelopes filled with money that Chinese people give to family and friends on special occasions such as weddings or the Chinese New Year. WeChat described its service as hongbao online, calling it WeChat Pay. Within a year, WeChat Pay had more users than Alipay. Alipay added a peer-to-peer payment feature a year later, but by that time, the damage was done. Alipay had lost its dominance. As figure 19 shows, by 2016, WeChat Pay had grabbed 38% of the Chinese payment market.

Could Alipay have stopped WeChat Pay completely? Probably not. But it could have avoided significant loss of market share if it had launched a peer-to-peer payment service more quickly. All companies must respond fast, as soon as their customers' needs change. Once a need arises, customers will buy the first available product or service to meet it well. This is true no matter how popular or innovative your product or service once was. To keep ahead of your competitors, you have to be constantly embracing change and launching new products before competitors do.

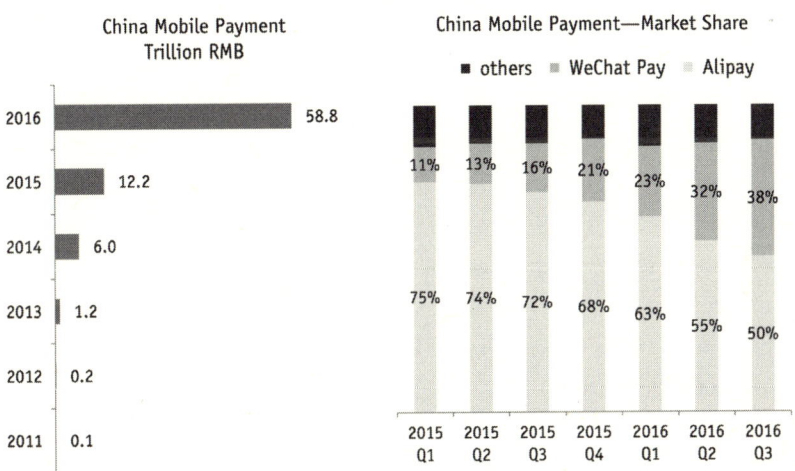

FIGURE 19 China mobile payment market. In 2016, the market was equivalent to $8.6 trillion. Sources: Market size from iResearch, embedded figure, in Tingyi Chen, "China Mobile Payment Report 2017," WalktheChat, June 25, 2017, https://goo.gl /b9KAE8; market share calculated from Analysys data, in "Alipay vs. WeChat Pay— Who Is Winning the Battle?," *ASEAN Today*, February 28, 2017, https://goo.gl/Yke9aJ.

AFTER LAUNCH, PLAN FOR QUICK SCALING
TO KEEP UP WITH DEMAND

Even companies that embrace change by innovating can lose their competitive advantage if they spend too much time doing R&D and not enough on getting their operations ready for launch. This is a common error. Companies don't plan for adequate capacity at their manufacturing site or at the suppliers' end.[3] Then the lack of capacity, or lack of flexibility in changing capacity to keep pace with fluctuating demands, ends up delaying delivery to customers. Competitors take advantage of the delay to catch up, and the innovating company loses out—all because it didn't prepare its operations for the launch!

Take a look at Boeing's struggle to meet the demand for the 787. As soon as the 787 was unveiled, in 2007, customers wanted it. The aircraft enabled point-to-point connections, unparalleled fuel efficiency, and all the passenger comforts that airlines were demanding. However, Boeing not only struggled to introduce the product but also took several years to deliver it to customers commercially. Its suppliers were not ready to meet the increased demand and, for one reason or another, Boeing had to ask its customers to wait. Airbus then developed its competitive product, the A350, in time to catch up with 787 deliveries.

The result was that Boeing missed its chance to dominate the new format in which it had invested so heavily. Now, to compete with Airbus, Wikipedia notes that Boeing is rumored to be losing millions of dollars on every 787 it sells. Had Boeing planned its operations better, it could have delivered on time (too quickly for Airbus to catch up) and increased both its revenues and it profits. Boeing unveiled the plane in 2007 but didn't start deliveries until 2011. From 2011 to 2015, deliveries increased from 3 to 135, whereas Airbus started A350 deliveries in 2014 and increased them to 78 by 2017. Deliveries of 787s have plateaued since 2015, while A350 deliveries have grown (figure 20).

Zara, a fast fashion company, understands the importance and implications of responding quickly to changing customer tastes. They get new catwalk trends to stores on time by speeding up the supply chain. How? They keep their manufacturing facilities close to the market

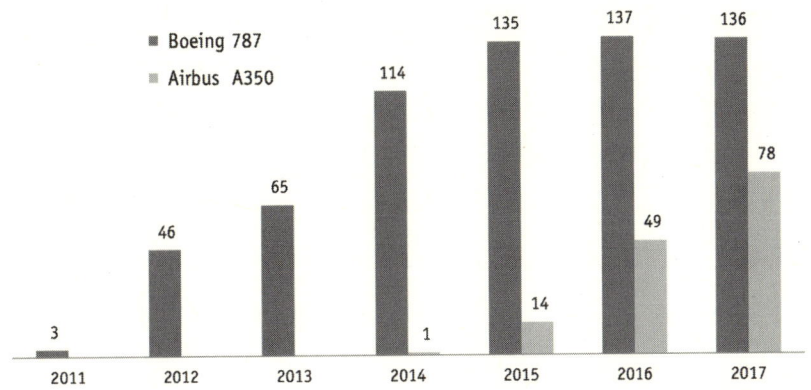

FIGURE 20 Boeing 787 and Airbus A350 deliveries. Source: "List of Boeing 787 Orders and Deliveries," and "List of Airbus A350 XWB Orders and Deliveries," Wikipedia, accessed March 22, 2019.

instead of locating them in distant Asian countries, so new designs reach stores within a week. They produce in smaller quantities, based on actual customer demand, and supply their stores twice a week. Only the less trendy clothes, like T-shirts, are outsourced to Asian countries.

The other advantage: because Zara updates its stock constantly, customers come in to check it frequently. It's estimated that customers visit a Zara store seventeen times a year—other stores average three visits a year.[4] Plus, since Zara produces in smaller quantities, it rarely marks anything down and thus has a greater profit. In fact, fast fashion stores offer fewer markdowns; the percentage is estimated to be 15%, compared to 30% for the rest of the apparel industry. Zara has seen phenomenal growth in Europe and now in the United States. Other apparel retailers are closing stores in the United States, but Zara is opening them.

However, it is the ability to deliver to customers quickly—not low prices—that drives success in the fast fashion industry, and that's true for other industries as well. The ability to quickly take your new products or services to market can make or break any business. Look at Airbus. It can introduce products and scale quickly because of its planning, which includes streamlined operations. Its modular design significantly simplifies its operations and allows it to scale as demand changes. It buys partly assembled products from suppliers and assembles them at its plant. Boeing still struggles with streamlining its operations—and so its time to market is longer and its costs are higher.

CREATE THE RIGHT SERVICE MODEL

When faced with changing customer requirements, it's vital to develop an effective model for servicing your new business. This ensures that your cost structure and pricing (unlike Boeing's) are appropriate for your new product or services. Getting this right will also stop your competitors from stealing your customers with lower-priced offerings.

Most companies don't get it right, though. They use their old service models for their new products, which rarely works. It would be like McDonald's offering burgers from grass-fed cows, on gluten-free buns, without raising its prices, and then making each one from scratch, without figuring out how to serve them fast enough. Customers might love organic burgers at low prices, but they wouldn't wait half an hour for them. They would go elsewhere—and even if they didn't, McDonald's would lose money on each burger served, as Boeing does on its 787s. Old service models won't meet new customer needs, as the service may not be optimal or its cost may be higher. New service models will meet the new needs better. Then, once those become popular, you need to fine-tune them to further reduce cost—fast, before your customers move to disruptors.

The information technology service (outsourcing) industry since the dot-com bust shows the perils of not adapting—and the opportunities that provides for disrupters. Until the early 2000s, the IT service market was dominated by big U.S. companies like IBM, CSC, EDS, and Keane. But soon after the dot-com bust, in the early 2000s, a few Indian upstarts, such as Infosys, began delivering IT services. They had skeleton staffs in the United States and outsourced programming, data warehousing, customer support, and the like to India, where workers were far less expensive. At first, only a few American customers dared to use these upstarts, but once companies realized how cost-effective they were, many began outsourcing IT to India.

The icons of the industry tried hard to deliver IT support from off-shore, too, but by then it was too late for them to catch up. Most went out of business, and today only once-mighty IBM remains in the IT service business—and even it is a fraction of its former size. Meanwhile, Infosys has consistently increased its revenue while maintaining its margins. From 2012 to 2017, IBM's Global Technology Services (GTS) revenue growth remained negative, between −2% and −10%, while Infosys revenue growth remained positive, between 6% and 11% (see figure 21). GTS and Infosys maintained similar gross margins, while GTS's gross margin remained between 37% and 39% and Infosys's gross margin was between 37% and 42%.

Companies are (understandably) too slow to recognize when their approach to client services is not working. It's hard, risky, and expensive

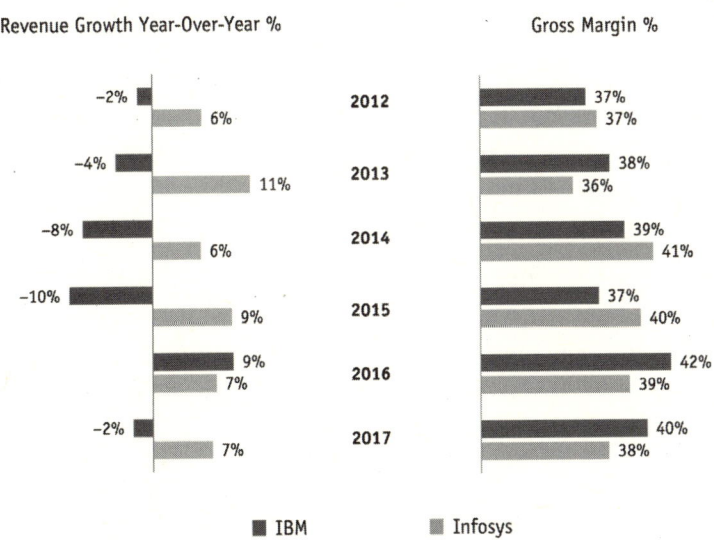

FIGURE 21 IBM Global Technology Services and Infosys revenue growth and gross margin. Sources: "Financial Reporting," IBM, https://goo.gl/vqwkWD; "Financials and Filings: Annual Reports," Infosys, https://goo.gl/yTyzFP.

to change the service model when it's seemingly performing well. So companies remain attached to their old models until they're so far behind that it's too late for them to catch up. That's what happened to the U.S. IT industry. To avoid their fate, you need to recognize when your old model is frustrating your customers—either in terms of its cost (as was the case with U.S. IT companies), of the service itself, or of its timing. And then you need to discard the old way of doing business and quickly come up with a cost-effective new one.

HOW TO RESPOND FASTER TO CHANGING CUSTOMER NEEDS

In the past, whether people were buying a product or a service, companies could keep the customer waiting and still keep their business. In restaurants, at checkout counters, or on the phone with a call center, customers waited. Those days are ending; we're all impatient now. If your products aren't available and someone else's are, your customers will buy from the competition.

This is even true for Apple, the company that commands more brand loyalty than almost any other. When the iPhone X shipment was delayed by two months, in 2017, Samsung was there with its Galaxy S9, and customers were too. The research firm Kantar says the iPhone X's delayed launch hurt iPhone's market share around the world.[5] If Apple's loyal fans won't wait, no one will.

Apple is still the largest company in the world in terms of market capitalization, but your company may not be so lucky if you make your customers wait. The concept should change from *What's the appropriate wait time?* to *What can we do to not make customers wait?* If customers can't wait a few seconds for an e-commerce site to load, there is no reason for you to design your service thinking they will wait for you. By making them wait, you are only frustrating them, and they will look for alternatives. Instead, design your service with no wait time, so your customers will leave *other* services for yours. Use their impatience to your advantage.

Here's how to get your products or services to them on time.

Step 1: Quickly Develop Products/Solutions That Address Customers' Changing Needs

As shown with Alipay, Boeing, and the whole U.S. IT industry, if a company doesn't address its customers' changing needs quickly enough, its competitors will, and those customers may never come back. It's much harder to win customers back once you've lost them than it is to keep them—and it costs more, too. Too many companies count on customers' loyalty. But being the first to design or offer something means nothing to customers if they can't get it from you when they want it.

Here's how to get a good enough handle on customer needs and be quick enough at developing new products to keep your customers.

Be a fast follower. Fast fashion wins with customers by closely following catwalk trends and what's selling in competitor's stores. They are never first with a fashion—sometimes they even get sued for blatantly copying competitors' designs. But their methods work. To emulate them, find the company that sets the standard in your industry and then quickly develop rival products without infringing upon their property rights. Think how other ride-sharing companies copied and improved upon Uber. There are parallels in all industries.

Keep an eye on proxies. In some industries, you have to watch for proxies to understand changing customer taste. The restaurant industry can provide excellent insights into changing tastes in food. If customers want healthier food in restaurants, they'll want healthier food at home too. Similarly, television shows are created based on successful movies. That's one reason why big studios like Disney own television stations.

Watch industry trends. Some customer preferences change slowly. In those industries, it's wise to be part of the trend rather than fighting it. For example, utilities' slow move to renewable energy is prompting wise players in the oil and gas industries to diversify. The Saudis are already doing it by moving some assets from oil and gas to other industries, like tourism. Companies such as BP, Shell, and ExxonMobil, on the other hand, are fighting the trend and keep investing everything in oil and gas—and are hoping that customers will keep wanting carbon-based fuel.

Follow global trends. Worldwide trends can be guides; what's popular in one country sometimes succeeds in another. Kao Japan created the Swiffer cleaning products and now Procter & Gamble sells them worldwide. Discount grocery chains such as Aldi, from Germany, spread throughout Europe and are starting to enter the United States. Yoga started in India and then became popular in the West, while Western gyms are gaining popularity in India. The best way to decide which international products will be successful in your local markets is to understand your customers' needs. For example, Patanjali products, made from herbs and plant chemicals, may appeal to U.S. millennials, whereas packaged food may not appeal to Indian customers, who desire fresh produce.

Trial and error. Sometimes none of the above apply to your industry. But there's one surefire method: come up with ideas and test them. Amazon does a great job of testing and perfecting an idea before launching it on a large scale. Many companies keep a close tab on start-ups in their space and then buy them out in the hope of catching the next big thing. Start-ups let companies test new ideas without significant investment, and the pharmaceutical and tech industries have profitably done this for years.

Step 2: Create New Service Models

Finding new ways to serve your customers once they have the new product or service is crucial. Even if they love the product or service itself, they may not continue to use it without a new service model to go with it. And using the old service model with the new product may not work for you, either. It's better to design a new service model, one that optimizes both performance and cost.

Consider corporate law firms. For the legal industry, the requirements of large corporations are changing. Corporations now want fixed fees and "all-you-can-eat" advice, and some even want it 24/7. The corporations say they're tired of negotiating every statement of work; they want their external lawyers to behave like in-house counsel, supporting their needs for a fixed fee. Some law firms pay their lawyers less than they did historically, while others allow fewer to become partners. Both are knee-jerk reactions that will be counterproductive in the long run.

It would be better for law firms to change how legal services are provided. For instance, if they created different service models for different situations—say, by using paralegals to review contract language and saving senior counsel for complicated issues—they could satisfy their clients' needs in ways that worked economically for the firm, too. So far, not many law firms are thinking this way, but if they don't, some upstart firm will. And that will completely disrupt the legal services industry.

Step 3: Speed Up the Supply Chain

A company can't react to changing customer preferences quickly unless its supply chain can also react rapidly. Too often, however, the supply chain becomes the bottleneck. When Steve Jobs returned to Apple as CEO, in 1997, he focused his talent on three problem areas: product pipeline, marketing, and supply chain. At that time, Apple had on hand two to three months' worth of supplier inventory and another two to three months' worth of finished goods inventory. Thus, Apple was projecting demand four to six months in advance of customer demand. Naturally, it was often wrong and couldn't respond to the real demands when they arose.

So Jobs hired Tim Cook to fix the problem. Cook replaced factories with contract manufacturers and cut back on warehouses and inventory, both of which reduced factory-to-customer lead time from months to days. Cook's efforts to improve Apple's supply chain were an undeniable factor in the company's financial success. Without Cook's supply chain, all of Jobs's design innovation and marketing savvy would have been wasted, because too many customers would have been waiting too long for the brilliantly designed and marketed products.

Although there can be no one-size-fits-all approach to speeding up supply chains, the suggestions that follow have helped many companies in many industries remove common bottlenecks.

Remove or reduce nonmoving inventory. The process of speeding up the supply chain starts with reducing or removing nonmoving inventory. A significant portion of most companies' inventory just sits in warehouses, occupying valuable space, clogging the system, and slowing down the supply chain. The nonmoving inventory ties up cash that could otherwise be used to generate revenue. Nonmoving inventory should be scrapped or deeply discounted. If neither is possible, move it out of the regular supply chain's warehousing and hold it off site to make room for goods that are selling. Even better, stop piling up nonmoving inventory by analyzing why it's not moving and developing strategies to fix the problems.

Simplify ordering. Customers can now order products in several ways: with their computers, through apps on their phones, or by phone calls. Everyone knows that these methods cost sellers less than retail stores, and that online orders cost less than call center orders. But did you know that online orders also are the most likely to be error free? Error rates increase as the number of people involved increases. Ordering errors cost time and money through confusion, incorrect shipments, and increased customer returns.

Simplify the network. Simplifying the supply chain by having separate supply chains for separate purposes can significantly speed things up. Companies could have separate supply chains for fast-moving, slow-moving, and nonmoving products. This separation may be at either the manufacturing or the supplier end, depending on the product and the demand for it. Simplification also could involve removing warehouses and simplifying the material flow.

Simplify delivery. The last mile of the supply chain—the delivery to customers—is both the most expensive and the most important for customer satisfaction. As we have said, customers won't wait. Companies could speed things up by delivering fast-moving products directly to the customer from the factory—or from the vendor, if manufacturing is outsourced. They could control costs by consolidating shipments of slow-moving items, as Ikea does when it delivers furniture to customers.

Flexible manufacturing. As we discussed in chapter 5, fast end-to-end delivery and personalization require flexible manufacturing, which can handle smaller lot sizes and faster changeovers.

Simplify supplier interactions. The interactions between a company's internal organization and external suppliers often create logistical and other problems that hamper the supplier's performance. Companies hire suppliers for their expertise, but many internal organizations, threatened by the supplier or not understanding its reasoning, force the supplier to follow their own procedures. Needless to say, this slows everything down and creates more problems. The solution is simple: let external organizations do the work, and hold them accountable for the output, but don't micromanage, and put in place plans that will facilitate cooperation and communication.

Reduce sales promotion. Most companies offer frequent sales promotions, in the mistaken belief that this is a good way to increase revenue and profits. They believe that, by doing so, they are triumphing over competitors, but actually they are borrowing from their own future. Sales promotions clog retailer shelves with inventory, and they don't work anyway; no one is going to brush their teeth fives time a day because a retailer is running a promotion on toothpaste! Even if a customer buys at the promotion price, the toothpaste company and the retailer make less profit on that toothpaste, while the customer simply delays his purchase of the next tube.

This is just as true for big-ticket items. Think about how car dealerships got clogged with compact and midsize sedans in 2017. Many had a ten-month backlog, because customers didn't want the cars. This kind of thing creates a ripple effect in the supply chain. Plants and suppliers have to build capacity for peak consumption, which sits idle during rest of the year. After the 2017 disaster, automotive companies stopped production for months and suppliers had to shut their plants for even longer.[6]

Another disadvantage of deep discounts is that it makes predictions about future buying patterns difficult. Companies can't accurately plan for the few days of buying frenzy, and products produced based on extrapolations from it have to be scrapped—or even discounted more deeply later. It's unrealistic to expect companies to get rid of sales promotions completely, but they would be wise to limit them to a few times a year, such as at Thanksgiving and Christmas (in the United States). And it's worth remembering that super-successful companies like Apple, Starbucks, and Trader Joe's never run sales promotions. Finally, discounting is a self-defeating incentive in the long term, because it can lead to customers buying your products *only* when they are deeply discounted.

Consider this real-life example of how speeding up the supply chain helped a consumer goods company, which we will call Derby. The company was promoting products like shampoos, soaps, and diapers in a developing market. Customers were unhappy because, although the new products were heavily advertised, they weren't always available in stores. Derby's sales channels were clogged with inventory left over from repeated sales promotions. The competition took advantage of all the excitement Derby had created and launched their own brands.

So Derby reduced inventory, streamlined its network, and reduced the number of warehouses—all of which sped up the supply chain. Derby then regained its market initiative and began launching products every month, with new products like toothpaste, cosmetics, and diapers contributing 50% to 70% of the next year's sales. Market share improved. Moreover, the productivity of the sales team rose by 30% to 50% as it focused more on selling new products than on pushing old ones to distributors and retailers.

Operationally, the cost of delivery declined from 75% of the sales price to 55%. Additionally, system inventory shrank from 115 days to 60 days. The percentage of perfect orders—meaning orders where the right quantity was delivered at the right time, with the correct billing—rose from 40% to 90%. At the same time, quality improved; the defect rate decreased from thirty thousand defects per million items produced to five thousand. Products were fresher when they reached customers, whose satisfaction with the company's product naturally increased. Retailers and distributors were happy to work with the company again.

Step 4: Produce Only What Your Customers Are Buying

Producing only what and as much as your customers are buying is always prudent. It keeps capacity available and prevents production and supply chain bottlenecks caused by overproduction. That's what Zara and other fast fashion companies do. They idle their plants when they don't have demand and refuse to produce products that are not selling. This gives them the capacity to make new products quickly.

Most companies don't do that. They mass produce in large quantities to keep costs down, believing that making more costs less. So operations teams are incentivized to keep the plants running even when the products aren't selling—and eventually get scrapped or deeply discounted.

These things happen because companies don't plan properly for production. They base their plan on forecasts created from history, not on present market trends. History can't predict the future. Statistically, forecasts are wrong as often as they're right. Too many things change—competitive action, customer taste or preference, disposable income—to predict customer demands based on past behavior.

Real-time demand information is a better guide. Shipping new products for the first time takes guesswork, but after that, you can base shipments on actual demand. That way, you use production capacities only for things that are actually selling. Even if demand data is not readily available, you can ask customers about future demand or orders. If that is not possible, then firms can estimate demand based on a customer's production plans and inventory levels. When selling to customers, then, companies can use actual order information instead of forecasts as a trigger for shipment and production. As demand information becomes more reliable, inventory can be reduced and capacity can be freed up for new product launches. The motto should be "Don't produce if the product is not selling." Otherwise, the product will occupy warehouse space, be either written off or sold at a discount, and dilute brand value.

RESPONDING FASTER TO CUSTOMER NEEDS

Customers are more impatient than they once were. Millennials want everything now and are impatient about everything from their careers to their purchases.[7] They have little brand loyalty and will embrace other products or services if their old favorites don't show up on time. This is true of millennials all over the world. Either you adapt to this mind-set or you lose to companies that respond to it quickly. And it's not just millennials; older generations are getting impatient too. They don't like to wait at a checkout counter or on the phone, and they won't wait for their favorite brands, either.

Leaders must figure out how to do things so that their customers don't have to wait. Otherwise, before they know it, their customers will be buying from their competitors. And, for most business leaders, doing things faster means thinking in entirely new ways, ways that match their customers' new expectations.

Let's see how Under Armour tried to do this. In 2018, the company was working on improving its operational efficiency by reducing inventory—and the corresponding number of SKUs. But speeding up the supply chain only benefits you if you have a product that your customers love. Otherwise, you're just reducing your costs without giving customers what they want. When their customers wanted fashionable workout clothes, Under Armour should have hired a fashion designer to create clothes customers could wear as casual, fashionable clothes—not just as athletic clothes. Then they should have kept experimenting and changing their designs based on what customers bought. Once they had done all that, it would have been smart to focus on producing smaller quantities, as fast fashion does. Instead, Under Armour only became more efficient at making what their customers didn't want.

A similar approach could help other companies to respond more quickly to customer needs. Tesla, for example, could have increased its output by thinking of its operations differently. Instead of producing everything in-house like other car manufacturers, it could have taken an approach similar to Apple's. Apple designs and markets its products but gets contract manufacturers to actually produce them. Similarly, Tesla could have designed and distributed the Model 3 and provided critical technology, such as the battery. Then, they could have asked another car manufacturer—one with experience in mass-producing low-cost cars—to make the Model 3. This would have been a win–win for both companies.

Following these steps will undoubtedly mean that companies like Under Armour and Tesla (and your company?) will have to change their design and operations completely. But these steps have brought many a company out of its death spiral and allowed it to begin its climb back to health and prosperity.

6

CUSTOMER-FOCUS STRATEGY 4: GOOD ENOUGH IS NO LONGER GOOD ENOUGH

QUALITY CAN BE A potent weapon, but only if you know how to use it. Most companies don't. As soon as they've beaten the competition, they consider themselves "good enough." But in today's world, no company—no matter how far ahead of the competition it is—stays good enough for long. Look what happened to McDonald's. Their growth has stalled, and Chick-fil-A is on its way to becoming the third-largest food chain in the United States by 2020.[1]

How did this happen? Chick-fil-A focuses on the kind of quality that today's customers care about. Their motto is "Food is essential to life, therefore make it good." They buy small birds that yield juicier meat and they have perfected its seasoning, hand-breading, and pressure cooking in 100% refined peanut oil. Their birds are raised in barns, not cages, on U.S. farms. They use only 100% real, whole breast of chicken, without fillers, added hormones, or steroids. By the end of 2019, the chickens will be raised without antibiotics. Most of their produce is freshly delivered to their locations.[2] Customers love spending on Chick-fil-A. An average location earns $4.4 million in revenue per year, compared to McDonald's $2.5 million—even though Chick-fil-A is closed on Sundays.

Good enough is no longer good enough in any industry. Even advertising and gimmicks as successful as McDonald's toys and Happy Meals are no longer enough to bring in customers. You have to give customers what they really want, and earn their trust. Millennials, Gen Z, and even some boomers trust peer reviews more than brands and advertising. These customers don't care what celebrities and advertisements say. When they want to know about product performance, quality, or service, all they have to do is look online. Their peers will tell them what they want to know—and answer their questions, too.

If a product has a problem, each peer review will describe the customer's experience with it, in detail, immediately. For example, Samsung's Galaxy Note 7 was a flagship smartphone that received excellent reviews from third-party reviewers before its launch. But some early customers reported that their phones caught fire or exploded within a few days of product launch in August 2016.[3] Social media spread the story—soon airlines were banning the phones or making passengers turn them off until they deplaned. Within a few months, Samsung had discontinued production and recalled 2.5 million phones, but when some replacement phones exploded or caught fire, too, Samsung's global market share for premium smartphones declined from 35% to 17%. During Samsung's debacle, the iPhone's market share jumped from 48% to 70% for premium products, and Chinese smartphone manufacturers like Huawei were quick to seize the opportunity to make significant gains as well.[4] So take quality seriously. If your products don't perform, your customers will find out from their peers—instantly—and your reputation may never recover.

To win with quality, set standards that customers can't resist and the competition can't beat, and then keep improving. Many companies make the mistake of thinking that quality means only the end product or service seen by the customer. Those who win with quality know better; they optimize their entire operations for quality. Customers may never see or smell Chick-fil-A's clean barns or see the way its employees handle the birds, but those things contribute as much as the cooking to what customers love about Chick-fil-A's delicious meals. Doing this kind of thing may mean challenging long-held perceptions in your company or industry. Do it anyway.

If you don't think your company needs to change, ask yourself these questions.

- How do customers view the quality of your company's products and services?

- How much importance does your company leadership attach to quality? Does leadership view quality as a game changer or as more of a placeholder?

- How hard do your internal organizations try to improve quality and delight customers?

Your company's survival depends on your answers to all three questions. In a world where peer reviews have more credibility than advertising or third-party endorsements, winners make every effort to improve quality. Doing that starts with getting honest feedback and then improving products in response to it. If your organization is dedicated to working with customers to set standards your competition can't meet, your company will wield the weapon of quality and will win. The steps in the process are described here; the specifics are up to you.

STEP 1: FOCUS ON QUALITY, NOW

Many U.S. companies got broadsided by high-quality Japanese products in the 1980s. But U.S. manufacturers (like those in the auto industry) didn't get the message. They remained convinced that they could compete on price. So they responded not with higher quality but with cost cuts and—when that failed—by getting imports restricted. Neither worked, and American manufacturing never recovered—not because American companies were paying their workers too much money but because American companies were paying too little attention to quality.[5]

Today, some U.S. companies have improved the quality of their products. However, it has come at a cost. GM, for example, lost to Toyota for a while, but GM is making quality vehicles now. It has won several JD Power awards, and test rides show that GM vehicles perform as well as any imported vehicles. But their vehicles are becoming expensive, and Toyota still outsells them.

So what's the answer? Whatever industry you're in, don't wait to focus on quality until a competitor does. Do it now, do it first, because your customers want it. A me-too offering later on may not get them back.

Quality Doesn't Have to Be Expensive

Millennials and others want only the best, but they don't want to pay premium prices for it—even for Apple products. Even though this is well known, however, many companies try to achieve the quality that customers expect and the standards that regulations demand by investing in expensive plants and equipment, which of course raises their costs. That's the wrong approach, and it doesn't work anyway.

To achieve quality without prohibitive costs, you have to think outside the box. When Tim Cook was asked why Apple products were so expensive, he replied, "Instead of saying, 'How can we cheapen the iPod to get it lower?' we ask, 'How can we do a great product and do it at a cost that enables us to sell it at the low price of $49?'" Some people wondered why Apple did not offer a Mac for less than a thousand dollars. Cook's response was, "Frankly, we worked on that, but we concluded that we couldn't do a great product. And so we didn't. But what we did do is we invented the iPad. . . . Now all of a sudden we have an incredible experience that starts at $329. Sometimes you can take the issue or the way you might look at an issue and solve it in different ways."[6] That's great advice, and the iPad was a great idea.

Other industries, too, are finding innovative ways to provide affordable quality. Look at discount food retailer growth in Europe. Most of us associate the word *discount* with low quality. However, discount food retailers in Europe adopted a different strategy to win customers. Two grocers, Aldi and Lidl, concentrated on offering fewer foods but at lower prices. Their first stores were small and had a low-cost feel, but customers kept coming, because they were getting better value there. Then, in 2000, Aldi and Lidl began offering higher-quality products at lower costs than the competition did. Their products beat branded products in both head-to-head tests and independent quality reviews. In customer surveys, shoppers indicated that Aldi's products were better than national brands in categories such as milk, eggs, canned goods, and frozen foods, despite the fact that their prices were significantly lower.

Since then, both companies have slowly expanded their product offerings to include packaged goods such as baby food, breakfast cereal, and even personal care and beauty care products. Customers typically started by trying a few products, such as eggs and milk, and then, once they were satisfied with their quality, quickly moved on to other products in the store.

Soon, people from all income levels, attracted by the higher quality, began patronizing the stores. The discounters opened bigger stores and offered more variety. Now they have fresh produce, baked goods prepared on site, and some organic and gluten-free choices in both categories. Many have refrigerated sections and the look and feel of other grocery stores. However, they are careful to offer a better shopping experience than the competition's: longer opening hours, faster checkouts, more space, and better lighting.

And with all this, discounters still kept their prices 15% lower than established-grocery private-label products and 50% lower than branded products.[7] They were able to do this because they worked with fewer products and a select number of food manufacturers, which—combined with their large volumes—allowed them to buy in bulk at favorable prices. Typically, Aldi and Lidl work with regional manufacturers, too—purchasing pasta from Italy, for instance—to get the best quality. And whenever they can do so without lessening quality, they remove operational costs.

Millennials drove the growth of discounters. They prefer discounters over regular grocers in most markets. Millennials, as discussed earlier, are not brand conscious. They inherently trust discounters more than regular grocers. Then, when discounters offered higher-quality products, a broader assortment, and improved shopping experience while maintaining lower prices, baby boomers and Gen Xers started visiting the stores.

These days, food discounters have taken over the grocery market in Europe. In Norway, Germany, and Denmark, they have captured a 50% market share. In other European markets, such as the United Kingdom, the Netherlands, Ireland, and elsewhere, they are proliferating. Discounters entered Ireland in 2000, and by 2015 they had a quarter of the market share (figure 22). Since Aldi and Lidl became big in the United Kingdom, regular grocers have seen their margins shrink from 5% to less than 3%. And the discounters kept growing. By 2017, Aldi had more than ten thousand stores in eighteen countries and more than €50 billion (about $56.5 billion) in revenue. Lidl had ten thousand stores in twenty-eight European countries.

Now discount grocers are starting to make a dent in the U.S. food retail market. Aldi opened its first U.S. location in 1976, in Iowa; by 2017 it had 1,700 stores, and it plans to open eight hundred more by 2022. Lidl opened fifty-three stores on the U.S. East Coast by the middle of 2018. With every expansion of discount grocery stores, U.S. customers benefit from higher-quality products. Are Whole Foods and other grocers with

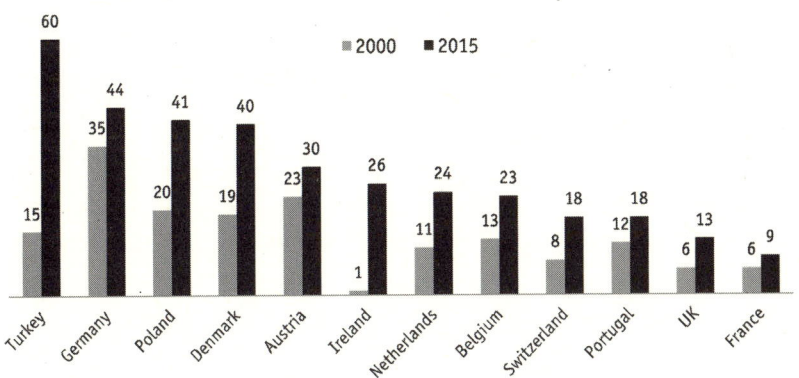

FIGURE 22 European discount grocers' market share (percent). Source: Planet Retail, embedded figure, in Rune Jacobsen et al., "How Discounters Are Remaking the Grocery Industry," BCG, April 11, 2017, https://goo.gl/7b9jvn.

high prices prepared to compete? Aldi and Lidl will likely take over the U.S. grocery market with higher quality and lower prices, a strategy that does better than the "everyday low prices" offered by Walmart.

Quality Is Essential for All Industries

Most people assume that "quality" refers only to products, but it applies to service, too, and companies in all industries provide examples.

Qatar Airways, for example, focused on quality and won business class customers from competitors who had been in the industry far longer than they had. Skytrax ranked Qatar Airways the world's best airline four times in the past seven years, and the airline has won numerous other awards, including World's Best Business Class and Best Airline Innovation. Even Qatar Airways Cargo won the Global Cargo Airline of the Year award.[8] Clearly, this airline takes quality seriously! It focuses on business passengers, offering them luxuries like space, high tech of all kinds, and seats that can recline to the point of complete flatness. First class is even more luxurious; some have said it's like flying in a private jet. In both first class and business class, Qatar passengers eat whenever they want—at their convenience, not the crew's. While other airlines are scrapping free meals, Qatar Airways is promising a "new age of airline dining." Service extends to the airport. Doha International is the world's sixth-best airport. It handles half as many passengers as JFK, yet 86.34% of its flights left on schedule.

Qatar Airways keeps raising the bar, and other airlines are finding it difficult to catch up. Despite blockades by neighboring countries in 2017, Qatar Airways grew revenue by 10.4% and profit increased by 21.7%.[9] However, none of this is enough in today's world. Even Qatar Airways, number one in the world, needs to keep improving or another upstart will slip in and start stealing its market share.

One way Qatar could improve is to offer its economy passengers more. If it doesn't, rivals who *do* offer their economy passengers more, such as Singapore Airlines, may start stealing Qatar's customers. Singapore Airlines has well-trained cabin crews in economy, and it serves excellent food and provides comfortable seats in that class. They know that all customers—rich or poor, old or young, from the third world or the first—appreciate quality.

It's not enough to be the best. Any company has to *stay* the best. In Qatar's case, that means serving its economy class as well as it serves its business class.

Quality Is in the Eye of the Beholder

Although all customers appreciate quality, their definitions of it differ. What's high quality to one segment may be mediocre to another. For example, business class passengers assume that they will have comfortable seating, clean bathrooms, palatable food, and respectful service during the flight. Given how most airlines treat their economy class passengers, most of them would be thrilled to have all these things. But Qatar doesn't bother; they don't train their economy class crews as thoroughly as they train the crews in business class. The food in economy is average at best. In the long run, this will hurt Qatar. Singapore Airlines treats its economy passengers so well that people are willing to pay a premium for it.

All businesses—not just airlines—need to meet the needs of all their segments; if they don't, their competitors will. Android devices are an apt example. In 2005, Google acquired Android and, because they were late to the market, made the platform free to all smartphone manufacturers to facilitate faster adoption. Millennials and tech-savvy customers loved how easy it was to customize Android devices—and how much better than the iPhones they were at taking pictures, using apps, typing, checking mail, and getting directions. While iPhones remain popular with boomers and not-so-tech-savvy individuals, Android appeals more to the younger generations.

Gartner estimated that Android had 54% of operating system share for all devices (mobile, laptop, and tablet) shipped by manufacturers worldwide in 2015. Apple's iOS and Windows had only 12% each.[10] Microsoft, realizing that its handheld devices had lost the quality war, eventually dropped its Windows Phone and now has no presence in the largest computing devices market, smartphones. Windows might have held on to its smartphone market if it had realized sooner that customers and manufacturers define quality very differently.

STEP 2: SET STANDARDS THAT CUSTOMERS CAN'T RESIST

Customers are thinking about their needs; most manufacturers are thinking about meeting regulatory standards. But regulatory standards are always a few steps behind evolving customer needs, so merely meeting regulatory standards is never enough. The United States has no regulations for internet companies, but Facebook is losing European subscribers and younger customers because of its violations of their privacy. Meanwhile, Apple is touting its respect for users' privacy and winning customers' trust. Similarly, while Washington is still debating whether global warming is real, millennials (and others) are demanding environmentally friendly products. So don't wait for regulations to make you change your standards. Think about quality from the customer's perspective, and then think about how you will raise and live up to your own new standards.

As we have discussed, customers' needs are changing continually. Don't become complacent. Push for improving standards that customers will value—standards that set you apart from the rest of your industry. For example, Southwest Airlines has the highest customer loyalty among all U.S. airlines, and they only serve economy customers. Customers rave about how well Southwest employees treat them and how easy it is to deal with them. This is because Southwest treats its employees well. It values its employees *and* its customers, and this keeps both groups happy.

Southwest employees do everything they can to make flying easy and entertaining—and all service industries ought to learn from them. If you are in a service industry, customers will judge you by how well your employees treat them. Apple, Google, Disney, Starbucks, and others are famous for quality because they make every effort to set standards that customers can't resist and then continue to improve on those standards. Successful business-to-business companies do the same.

But most companies look at the value of quality improvement very differently. They see it only from their own perspective and not from the customer's perspective. For example, biological and particulate contamination is a significant concern for medical patients. Though the medical devices industry has addressed biological contamination, small particles remain a source of enormous waste within the pharma world and represent a substantial risk in patient care. If any company could significantly reduce or eliminate particulate contamination, it would gain a significant competitive advantage, because the risk to patients of developing severe allergic reaction due to particles would be significantly reduced.

Even so, medical devices companies thought particle-free products would be impossible to make. But one of our clients, a small company we'll call MediDevi, which made caps for medicine vials, decided to try. When a vial became contaminated, nurses usually noticed small particles in the fluid and discarded the whole vial. This cost pharmaceuticals millions of dollars in lost drugs and product recalls—and all because of a cap that cost a few cents!

MediDevi used a mechanical process developed decades ago to produce the caps, and the company had been getting complaints about tiny particles in its caps—plastic, lint, dirt, or hair that stuck to the caps, sometimes contaminating whatever was in the vial and sometimes causing allergic reactions in patients. In addition, discarded drugs and pharmaceutical product recalls were costing millions of dollars. After the MediDevi sales organization discussed with pharmaceutical companies the benefits of better caps, they decided to try to develop caps that would keep the vials particle free.

MediDevi realized that caps that kept vials particle free could be a game changer in the industry. They asked our firm to compute the value and costs of reducing particulate contamination. Using medical research and reports from the Food and Drug Administration, we realized that reduced compliance risk (recall) and rejection rates would more than make up for the increase in costs that a particle-free manufacturing and supply chain would incur. The benefit varied with the drug price—the more expensive drugs would see higher benefits (see figure 23). Our analysis estimated that the rubber cap cost would increase by 42% for the expensive drugs but that the reduced compliance risk rate (269% of the cap cost) and filling rejection rate (73% of the cap cost) would more than make up for it.

Benefits from reduced inventory holding and processing costs were marginal, but overall we found that the company would save 315% of the rubber cap cost. In other words, if the pharmaceutical company was spending $10 million on the rubber cap before quality improvements, the rubber cap cost would go up by $4.2 million but they would save $31.5 million because of the improved quality. We estimated the overall benefit to be 185% for medium-price drugs and 41% for low-price drugs.

However, MediDevi's supply chain organization did not understand the benefits at first. They were incentivized to reduce cost and increase throughput but had no incentive to reduce particulate contamination. And if they focused on removing particulate contamination, they'd have to change the fundamental design of their plants,

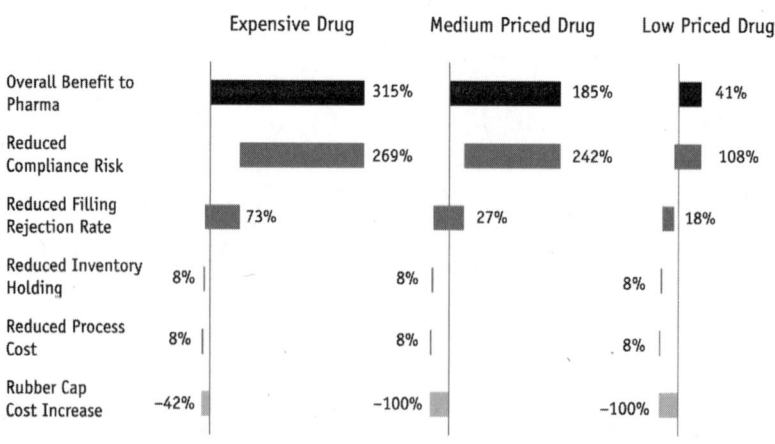

FIGURE 23 Benefit to pharmaceutical companies of reduced particulate contamination, expressed as a percentage of rubber cap cost. Source: Three S Consulting.

which were designed to produce as much as possible, not to provide the highest quality. Even so, MediDevi insisted on the changes, persisted, and achieved the impossible: contamination-free caps. Customers couldn't stop ordering, MediDevi's revenues soared, and the competition found it difficult to match MediDevi's higher quality. Competitors had to deal with significant rejections and found the process unsustainable.

STEP 3: OPTIMIZE MANUFACTURING FOR QUALITY, NOT OUTPUT

Most manufacturing operations are like the medical devices industry in valuing throughput over quality and in following a century-old system of quality control. Though quality control is part of the manufacturing process, it's almost always an afterthought; inspection is done only at the end of each stage. The design philosophy is focused on squeezing as much production out of a plant as possible. The objective is to lower costs. Thus, many low-quality products are made, on the assumption that any falling below minimum standards will be rejected during the inspection and then discarded or fixed.

However, relying on inspections at the end of the production process and doing checks at each stage can lead to defective products. And as the exploding Samsung Galaxy shows, even a small number of lemons can kill a flagship product and dent a company's reputation for good. In addition, inspecting every single product costs too much to be practical, even when the inspection process is automated. Even so, any poor-quality product that inspection misses can lead to a product recall or a bad review on Amazon or social media. The effects of recalls and bad reviews last a long time.

The philosophy should be that no poor-quality products will ever be produced, period. This requires a different manufacturing mentality. It means redesigning your manufacturing process so that you only produce products that meet your new high-quality standards. This is completely different from relying solely upon inspections at the end of the process—but it's time to make the change, no matter how difficult or expensive it seems in the short term.

That's what MediDevi did. A series of experiments showed them that once contamination had entered the manufacturing process, it was impossible to get rid of it, even with state-of-the-art equipment such as clean rooms. So they ended up completely changing their manufacturing process, and that finally resulted in particle-free caps.

MediDevi learned a lesson that few companies master: you have to fix quality problems at the source of the problem, not at the end of the process. That's the only method that works. In MediDevi's case, the clean room environment at the end of the manufacturing process did little to reduce contamination levels (figure 24). Our experiments showed that the number of particles larger than 25 microns in size (in a 10 square centimeter area) was two in molding, seventeen in cutting, twenty-one in washing, and nineteen in final washing. There were two insights from the experiments: first, that the cutting process introduced contamination, and second, that the washing processes didn't remove these particles and in fact ended up increasing them. MediDevi had to stop the contamination that was entering during the cutting and washing processes.

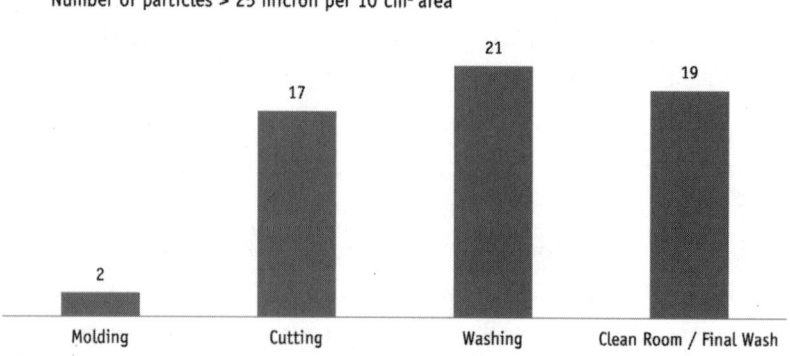

FIGURE 24 Particulate contamination after each production stage. Source: Three S Consulting.

Once they changed the cutting and washing processes, MediDevi found that optimizing production for quality actually reduced costs, because significantly fewer caps had to be discarded and inspections took so much less effort. MediDevi pleased its customers, outstripped its competition, and increased margins by focusing on quality.

But most companies today aren't making this change in thinking. They continue to focus production on throughput. They still believe that the more they produce, and the lower the production costs, the more they will please customers. That's no longer true. Focus on throughput results in poor-quality products that run the risk of recall and negative reviews. The cost of low quality is high. A better approach is to optimize manufacturing for quality so that products consistently meet quality standards. Producing high-quality products with zero rejection rates can be surprisingly cheap. It makes no financial sense to optimize manufacturing for output.

STEP 4: DON'T BE AFRAID TO CHALLENGE INDUSTRY NORMS

Manufacturing processes in most companies are set up to follow industry norms, which rarely improve quality standards. Even if following industry norms (or whatever the industry is doing to set standards) works for a while, staying competitive requires a company to continually evaluate its standards against changing customer needs. Instead, most stick with manufacturing processes that can't produce products that measure up to their customers' new needs. Then, if they realize that they're not meeting the new needs, most merely automate their old systems rather than using their customers' requirements to design new systems.

For example, the MediDevi manufacturing process mirrored their pharma customers' manufacturing requirements, with clean rooms and garments, at a significant cost. Pharma customers loved the manufacturing process. However, it did nothing to improve quality or reduce particulate contamination. What worked for pharma customers didn't work for their suppliers. When MediDevi first tried to solve the contamination problem, therefore, they sent a team to inspect a counterpart in Japan. The team came back with a recommendation to invest in a new high-tech automated facility—at a cost of millions of dollars—but initial results did not show any significant improvement in quality. MediDevi already produced better quality caps than their Japanese counterparts or fully automated manufacturing. MediDevi had to think outside the box to improve quality.

As they worked through the problem, many widely accepted industry standards were found to be of little value. Washing with water is a traditional cleaning process in the pharma industry. However, analysis showed that washing was appropriate for biological contamination but increased particulate contamination—rubbing during washing created more particles. So MediDevi tried changing the last cleaning step from water to air drying. That removed smaller particles more efficiently. Similarly, commonsense improvements such as requiring employees to wear gowns and to follow simple hygiene and cleaning practices reduced particulate contamination just as well as the very expensive, industry-norm clean room did. At first, MediDevi's manufacturing team resisted these changes because they were so radically different, but once they tried them and saw the results, they were convinced. And their customers loved the contamination-free caps.

If challenging industry norms will improve the quality of your products, make the changes. It will be difficult for regulators or customers to argue with the results—and for competitors to catch up with you.

STEP 5: THINK SUPPLY CHAIN

Historically, companies have measured and tested quality only within their own four walls. For example, Toyota, Honda, and other car manufacturers focused on the quality of their in-house manufacturing but didn't subject the air bags sent to them by Takata to rigorous enough testing—a fatal error. Twenty people in Honda cars died when the Takata air bags exploded upon inflation.[11]

Any chain is only as strong as its weakest link—and that's as true for supply chains as for any other kind. Product quality has to be strong all along the chain, as Takata's failure shows. The exploding air bags put the reputation of Toyota, Honda, and several other auto manufacturers at risk. Honda executives had to testify before Congress, cut their profit forecast by more than $400 million due to recall-related costs, and ask their CEO to step down.

To achieve higher quality standards, it's not enough for companies to maintain standards in their own plants—they have to work with their suppliers and customers. MediDevi found that even all the improvements at their own plants couldn't reduce contamination until their pharmaceutical customers changed their processes. The pharmaceutical companies opened and inspected all incoming products, including of course the caps. Then they tested and washed the caps before putting them on their vials. So all the benefits of producing cleaner caps were lost when their cartons were opened and exposed to unclean warehouses. The only way to keep the caps clean was to put them straight into the pharmaceutical companies' manufacturing process, without inspections. This was a significant change for the pharmaceutical companies, and some didn't agree with it. As a compromise, MediDevi proposed sending samples via FedEx for testing, a compromise that worked for both parties.

Over the course of two years, the optimization and changes to the manufacturing process reduced contamination by a factor of one hundred. MediDevi opened a whole new market with the high-quality product and its associated revenue source. Due to the drop in throughput, the cost for the client increased, but their customers were more than happy to compensate them. Overall cost reduction and patient benefits were immeasurable. Competitors tried to copy the visible changes in machinery and process but failed to fine-tune the overall process to achieve MediDevi's higher quality standards. MediDevi won because they focused on their customers' needs and had the courage to make big changes all along the supply chain.

It's impossible to improve quality by focusing only on your own operations. You can achieve higher levels of quality only by considering customers and suppliers as part of your manufacturing system.

WINNING WITH QUALITY

As we discussed earlier, more and more customers are reading peer reviews on Amazon and other sites before buying products or services. They're looking at product performance, service, and quality issues, and they believe what their peers tell them—not companies' claims or advertising. In this environment, all products and services are judged on their own merit, according to how well they work for customers. Improving quality is a sure way to get repeat business and to attract new customers with favorable reviews.

Despite how well known all this now is, however, corporate leaders continue to use quality as a placeholder. As long as they're doing as well as the competition in quality, they focus on other strategies to improve stock price. Some companies, such as Volkswagen and Takata, have even been caught lying to their clients and to regulators about quality performance. It's hard for a company—even one as well loved as Volkswagen used to be—to win back its reputation and customer trust after something like that. Volkswagen sales have yet to regain their prescandal levels.

Other companies—such as discount grocers and international airlines—are wielding quality as a weapon and using it to win customers from competitors. These companies have disproven the myths that higher-quality products cost more and that automation somehow improves quality. Discount grocers have shown that higher quality can be achieved at lower prices. Many high-volume, low-cost wines are winning with quality, because producing in quantity can ensure consistency and higher quality levels.

And customers find out about quality not through expensive advertising but through peer reviews. These are very different from professional reviews, and they change far more frequently. Take, for example, noise-canceling headphones. They are becoming popular as more and more people are using them to listen to music in planes, in open offices, and even while mowing lawns. Bose and Sony are the leading manufacturers, with similarly priced products. Third-party reviewers consistently rate Sony higher than Bose in sound quality and features.

However, customer reviews on Amazon tell a different story. Customers prefer Bose because Sony headphones break easily—and when they do, no one is willing to spend another $300 on them. Bose headphones don't break and are more comfortable, though the sound quality is not as good as Sony's. Sony is trying to catch up, but Bose keeps getting better, not only keeping its current customers but also attracting new ones with new features like Alexa voice control. That's what you have to do to win with quality: keep improving standards to keep delighting your customers.

7

CUSTOMER-FOCUS STRATEGY 5: DISREGARD STRATEGIES 1 THROUGH 4

W HAT MAKES YOU GREAT today won't necessarily keep you great tomorrow, unless you and your strategies evolve with your customers. That applies even to strategies 1 through 4 in this book. Continuing to follow them even when your customers' needs change could be your undoing. Everything depends on your customers and how much attention you pay to their needs. As those needs change, your strategies may need to change, too. Some of the companies profiled here, like GE, IBM, or Coca-Cola, or in behemoth business bestsellers like *Good to Great* or *In Search of Excellence* are struggling or are on the verge of dying because they took their focus off their customers and stopped reinventing themselves.

Jeff Bezos said, "If your customer base is aging with you, then eventually you are going to become obsolete or irrelevant. You need to be constantly figuring out who are your new customers and what are you doing to stay forever young."[1] Great companies focus on their current *and* future customers' needs. Delighting current customers is not enough. You have to wow them in the future—and your new customers, too, whoever they may be. Unless you're continuously evolving, you'll die. That's why so few companies (less than 1%) founded more than one hundred years ago still exist today. They didn't evolve with their customers.

It's hard to predict the future in anything, especially when it comes to customers who keep changing what they want. The only way to do it is to become skilled at creating strategies that support your customers' needs—and then to keep updating those strategies. You can only do that if your whole organization is set up to identify and respond to customers' needs as, and even before, they arise.

The strategies discussed so far in this book won't work if you follow them only once. You need to keep revisiting and revising them—and have the courage to start over completely to *keep delighting* your customers. This is hard for most companies. They don't change, even when they are losing large numbers of customers. Only a few companies have mastered the art of evolving with changing customer preferences and doing it consistently.

Consider Disney. Mickey Mouse, Donald Duck, and Disney feature-length cartoons like *Cinderella* were hugely popular in the 1940s, 1950s, and 1960s. But even by the late 1950s, kids were not as into these cartoon characters, so Disney developed movies like *Old Yeller* and *The Parent Trap*, and they too were popular (and remain popular with boomers). And as tastes continued to change, Disney changed right along with them, winning over Gen Xers and millennials by purchasing Pixar in 2006, Marvel Entertainment in 2009, and Lucasfilm, with its *Star Wars* and Indiana Jones franchises, in 2012. Marvel and *Star Wars* became the two highest-grossing movie franchise of all time. And Disney was also careful to keep Disneyland up to date, not only by adding new attractions but also by executing well. Seventy percent of those who visit Disney theme parks return.

Very few companies evolve as well as Disney did. As we've mentioned, only 1% of U.S. companies survive for one hundred years or more. And even the survivors are having a hard time maintaining momentum and appealing to the young. Disney is unique in its ability to keep reinventing itself and to keep delighting its customers.

To see if your company is like Disney in this regard, ask yourself these questions.

- How does your company plan to delight future customers? What needs will you address and what strategies will you use?

- What organizational capabilities do you have that will help you identify and respond to customers' future needs?

If you can't immediately start listing answers to both questions, your company will eventually lose customers and market share—no matter how successful it may be now. Whatever products or services you provide, the only way to stay successful is to keep delighting customers, and to do that you need to keep evolving strategies and to make everyone in the company aware of their importance.

To execute those strategies, empower your frontline team to do right by your customers, and pay attention to detail throughout your organization. That's what Disney has always done. It understands future customer needs enough to keep delighting both old and new customers, empowering teams to help customers and paying attention to detail everywhere.

Unless you change your mind-set and do these three things, too, you won't evolve—you'll die.

UNDERSTANDING FUTURE CUSTOMER NEEDS AND DEVELOPING STRATEGIES FOR THEM

Customers today are quick to develop new needs and to let old ones go, and it's tough to keep up, to see not only what they want but what they *will* want. What's hot today is never so hot tomorrow. If they're still buying the same general kinds of products and services you provide, you can respond quickly enough, as we showed in chapter 5. But what if your customers change and want something completely different—something you don't even offer?

That's what happened to dairy farmers who focused on organic milk. You would imagine that organic milk products would be popular with millennials, and they were, at first. Health-conscious customers drove the consumption of organic milk, and sales volume grew by 22.5% from 2010 to 2015.[2] This led producers to expand capacity and increase prices. But then customers decided that almond and coconut milk were healthier and cheaper. The market became glutted with organic dairy products, and the price per hundred pounds declined from $40 in 2016 to $27 in 2017. And consumption continued to fall. In the fifty-two weeks ending November 25, 2017, organic milk sales declined by 2.5% while sales of specialty milk and milk substitutes increased by 10.5% and 2.9%, respectively (figure 25).

Customers all over the world are making the same kinds of sudden shifts in what they want. Of the top one hundred Chinese brands in 2007, as reported by *Fortune,* only forty-six remained top brands in 2018.[3] Some companies manage to keep up with customers' changing tastes and thrive. They do that by identifying future trends and developing strategies to deliver on them.

However, most companies and leaders are not good at recognizing what their current customers want, let alone what customers' future needs will be. Companies may use market research and in-house discussions to come up with new strategies, but few of those connect with actual customer needs. Many companies make the mistake of creating an online presence rather than trying to figure out what their customers actually need or what will wow their customers in the future.

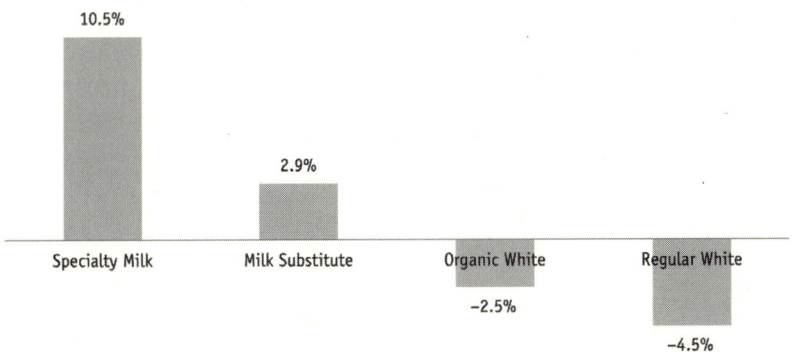

Specialty milk = lactose-free, etc.
Milk substitute = almond, rice, soy and other plant-based milks

FIGURE 25 U.S. milk sales growth for the fifty-two weeks ending November 25, 2017. Source: Neilsen, embedded figure, in Heather Haddon and Benjamin Parkin, "Dairies Are Awash in Organic Milk as Consumers Jump to Alternatives," *Wall Street Journal,* January 3, 2018, https://goo.gl/nG97eV.

However, some companies get it right. Haier, a Chinese manufacturer of home appliances and consumer electronics, has been identifying their customers' future needs for decades.

Zhang Ruimin, once a poor boy in a rural Chinese village, took over the company in 1984. Zhang challenged the status quo every few years and has completely reinvented the company several times since then.[4] He began by improving the quality of the products, because he understood that customers were unhappy with shoddy goods and that Haier desperately needed to become a quality leader. But he also understood that, for the company to succeed in this, his employees had to feel as ashamed of the shoddy goods as he did. So he had them smash seventy-six defective refrigerators—in public, in the street outside the factory. That was the first reinvention.

The second focus was on innovation driven by customers. Zhang realized that many segment-specific needs were not being met by what the company was selling, such as generic washing machines and refrigerators. Zhang decided to identify specific segments' unique unmet needs and to sell customized solutions to each.

The third reinvention focused on meeting customers' changing needs quickly. Zhang believed that Haier's lack of customer awareness was leading to delays and guesswork about new product manufacturing volumes. He created empowered teams that worked directly with customers and had the authority to manage resources.

When Zhang realized that customers were looking for products that could learn about and adapt to their environment, the company's fourth reinvention began. Haier introduced products like heating and cooling systems for children's rooms that change the temperature based on the child's activity (such as whether the child is playing or sleeping).

Each reinvention has been hugely successful, and Zhang's efforts completely transformed a small-town, bankrupt company into a global giant. Haier has had the largest market share of global household appliances in the world since 2011, and enthusiastic customers almost everywhere. From 2009 to 2017, Haier's share of the global household appliances market increased from 5.1% to 14.2% (figure 26).

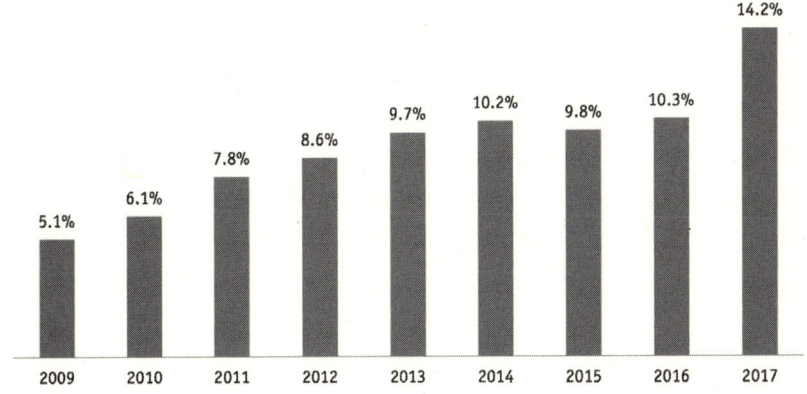

FIGURE 26 Haier's share of the global household appliances market. Source: "Haier Tops Euromonitor's Major Appliances Global Brand Rankings for Seventh Consecutive Year," Haier, January 22, 2016, https://goo.gl/xxsEY2.

As the transformation of Haier shows, successful businesses keep reinventing themselves as their customers' needs change. Identifying future customer needs is the most challenging part of this process. Since most companies don't look beyond what customers actually tell them, identifying future customer needs is difficult for them.

Two methods for identifying customer needs have worked well for my clients: 360 triangulation and partner workshops. Which to use depends upon who is directly involved in delivering goods or services to customers. If all responsibility lies in-house, 360 triangulation is best. If a third party will be responsible for any good or service delivered directly to customers, partner workshops are best. Even when partners lack strategic knowledge, they still can provide unique and valuable insights. Whether you triangulate or hold workshops, participation from partners, suppliers, and customers is crucial.

360 Triangulation

Those from outside the company—customers, suppliers, and stake-holders—see things from a different point of view than those inside the company and thus are a big help in figuring out future directions. When a leading coffee retailer hired our team to help them decide which kind of plastic cup to use, we worked with everyone involved, including the company's suppliers, to see what the customers really wanted and what would work.

As a first step, we needed a deeper understanding of the challenges faced by the retailer. We started by interviewing the leadership team, key partners, and suppliers. It became clear that the plastic cup suppliers couldn't deliver what the coffee company wanted (the supplier lacked the capacity) and that the coffee company's customers didn't like the fact that the plastic cups couldn't be recycled. It was obvious to us that the current plastic cups were never going to work. We had to find another solution.

Next, we spoke with researchers and experts in the field. Such people can provide excellent, and more objective, insights into where the market is heading. Our discussion showed that there were significant supply issues with the current cups and that alternative products could meet the retailer requirements just as well, if not better.

So we spoke with suppliers, who are an excellent source of information and insights. Because they spend time with competitors and other companies in the industry, suppliers can provide valuable insights into where the market is heading. In addition, because they are the ones who will have to support the changes, they're an excellent sounding board for different proposed solutions. Discussions with them revealed that they had a different plastic cup in development that might meet the retailer's needs. The new cup wasn't recyclable either, but it would significantly reduce the landfill impact as it contained less plastic.

However, when we circled back with the client team, the marketing organization came out vehemently against the new cups. They said that since the new cups weren't as clear as the old ones, customers would think they were dirty. They said their market research showed that customers wanted clear cups that looked like glass.

So we showed customers both cups and interviewed them. The customers saw no difference in the two cups' clarity but loved the environmental story of the new ones. As a result, the retailer launched the new cups—quickly, with a big marketing push. They were a huge hit, and even ten years later, the retailer is still using the cups for its summer beverages.

An approach like the one we took with the coffee retailer usually works well (though not always, as we'll see). Customers in general may or may not be able to guess at their future needs, but if they are asked the right questions, they usually can articulate their current needs. They may not be able to imagine what product or services will meet those needs, but they usually can say something simple about what they want—healthy foods, safe travel, or easy-to-use apps, for instance. They certainly can tell you how satisfied they are with the products or services currently available, and what they say about that gives a good perspective on what might succeed in the future.

Sometimes you need to look at changing customer preferences in other parts of the world, too. For example, when Japanese consumers started using their Sony phones to play music and watch videos, Nokia should have noticed. Their U.S. partners did—the wireless companies kept telling Nokia that people wanted music, videos, and cameras on their phones.

But Nokia—once number one in the world when it came to mobile phones—didn't see that the popularity in Japan of phones with data predicted their popularity in the United States and Europe, even though the Japanese had been the first to adopt other new apps and devices that later became big elsewhere. Nokia completely missed the increasing popularity of the data applications that later drove smart-phone innovation. If Nokia had triangulated with their partners, they would have noticed. But they didn't; they kept focusing on what had been so successful for them in the past: voice calls and miniaturization. And so they lost out to Apple. They never recovered.

360 triangulation is a powerful tool for visualizing customers' future needs, but it's far from a one-time exercise. The market changes so often, and so quickly, that companies need to triangulate every year. Only then will they have accurate ideas about whether they should stay on course, tweak their approach, or change direction.

Partner Workshops

If companies are dependent on suppliers or other partners to deliver goods and services directly to customers, then those partners need to be involved when a company is contemplating any change. Internal managers often push back on the idea of including outsiders, because they think suppliers lack strategic perspective, but partner inclusion is crucial because the partners will have to execute any strategy devised by the company. It makes sense to get their input sooner rather than later. Besides, if partners are involved in identifying future customer needs, they'll be far more likely to buy in to future strategies. Whether or not they agree with the need for change or its urgency, their inputs—especially their insights into the implications of change— are valuable.

For example, our firm was engaged by a large Canadian bank to restructure its IT outsourcing relationship. The outsourcing firm managed day-to-day customer interactions and played a crucial role in customer satisfaction. Customers routinely complained about not being able to access their accounts and about how long they had to wait on the phone or in branches. Both stemmed largely from the bank's reluctance to revamp its IT infrastructure, due to the signif- icant change and financial commitments that entailed. However, if the bank did not make a substantial change, it ran the risk of losing customers.

We decided to use a series of workshops to share with potential IT outsourcing firms the challenges facing the bank, to solicit proposals, and then to select the firm that would best meet future customer needs.

The purpose of the first workshop is for managers of the com- pany to give potential partners a complete picture of the current situation. Giving this picture may well involve tours of facilities, visits to branches and call centers, and sharing data on customer complaints. At some point, there needs to be an open forum during which partners may ask questions about the company's current state, the challenges it's facing now, and where it's expecting to go in the future. Internal attendees should ask questions about the potential partner's capabilities and solicit their perspectives on fixing customer's problems.

As a follow-up to this first workshop, partners should be encouraged to submit their own proposed solutions and guidance on costs. By end of this process, the company should have a high-level understanding of how they and their potential partners are envisioning their future direction, and some ideas about how they will get there. After the first workshop at the bank, some IT outsourcing firms proposed revamping the technology at the branches and call centers, while others suggested focusing more on apps and reducing reliance on branches.

At the second workshop, company and partner teams work together to assess the viability of each of the partner's proposed solutions. From the company's perspective, this workshop highlights different solutions that could potentially lead to an excellent solution for their customers. From the partner's view, the workshop provides an opportunity to gather feedback about their customer and the current situation, which helps them refine their thinking.

When the bank and their IT partners had their second workshop, it became clear that the bank first needed to think about which service model would work for customers and then decide about the supporting IT infrastructure. The service model had changed. Branches and call centers were no longer customers' preferred way to interact with the bank. Thus, the bank realized, it should be investing in smartphone apps and conveniently located ATMs, and its IT investment would have to be prioritized to support changing customer needs.

After the second workshop, the internal team gathers to critique various solutions proposed by the potential partners and to narrow the field to the ones they think are viable. Then the team shares these ideas with different stakeholders and the leadership team for feedback and refinement. At this stage, the team selects one or two partners for further discussion.

When the bank's internal teams met, they agreed that their current IT partner probably wasn't a good fit for the new direction. However, because the IT firm had legacy knowledge, they decided to invite their old IT partner to the third workshop, along with the potential new IT firm.

The purpose of the third workshop is to jointly refine the narrowed-down solutions based on feedback from stakeholders at both companies. At the workshop, nitty-gritty issues like the delivery plan, roles and responsibilities, and the governance model are refined. A partner is selected at this stage and is asked to provide final pricing for the refined solution.

After the third workshop, the bank decided to invest in apps and ATM infrastructure while reducing investment in branches. It chose to work with the new firm for this while using the current provider to maintain current branches and call centers. Eventually, as the bank reduced its branches and call centers, all the work would move to the new provider.

It often works out this way. After—or during—the workshops, a company and its current partners may realize that they can't work together on future solutions. If that happens, they can then work out a transition plan that allows a new company to enter into the mix while the current partner retires or takes a smaller role. Doing this as part of a joint, open process can make the change less emotional and painful for everyone involved, as the reasoning behind the decision should be clear to everyone. At the bank, for example, everyone worked together to develop a transition plan for the current IT provider.

After either triangulation or joint partner workshops, companies should continue to keep an eye on changing customer needs and keep tweaking their plans. Some of our clients have found it useful to have artificial intelligence systems keep an eye on changing customer preferences, update management on a regular basis, and monitor how well the new strategy is working. But it's important to remember that this follows the triangulation and partner workshops—it's not and never should be a substitute for them. Companies have to keep doing 360 triangulation or partner workshops every year or two to ensure that they are on top of their future customer needs.

Create New Business Strategies to Support Future Needs

Once companies have defined future needs, the next step is to create business strategies to support them and to thrill your customers. Haier provides a good example of changing business strategies to execute reinventions.

First, to improve the quality of Haier's products, Zhang created a joint venture with the Swiss company Lieber, to use and adapt their technology and quality practices at Haier. These practices included methods for continuous improvement and linked worker pay with quality performance. The focus on quality went beyond manufacturing; it was expanded to low inventory, short delivery times, and low working capital. The emphasis on quality enabled the company and its employees to develop the confidence to introduce more significant changes later.

For the second reinvention, ten years later, Zhang focused on meeting unmet customer needs through close collaboration among research and development, marketing, and sales teams. Working together, they created products like a vegetable washing machine; a compact, low-energy washing machine that could fit into a small apartment; and mini refrigerators for U.S. dorm rooms.

The third reinvention, in the 2000s, focused on a new program called "create zero distance with the customer." Zhang reorganized the organization around independent operating units, creating empowered teams to work with, and organizations to support, customers. Haier's eighty thousand or more workers are now organized into two thousand self-managed teams called *zi zhu jing ying ti* (ZZJYTs). The teams work directly with customers and manage their own profit and loss, hiring, and operating responsibilities. Employees are encouraged to come up with ideas, and the best are voted on by employees, suppliers, and customers. Those who come up with winning ideas became leaders of new ZZJYTs. Managers become service providers, giving team members both resources and guidance.

Now, for its fourth reinvention, Zhang is trying to use the internet to provide products that adapt to a customer's home and environment.

Haier launched an air conditioner, based on wind tunnel technology, that keeps air cool but not cold, which is what most Asians prefer. It is called Tianzun (Heaven).[5] The air conditioner can be controlled via smartphone, and it doesn't make any noise or change the moisture content of the air. This is just one of Haier's many intelligent home devices. Zhang is determined to lead on that. Haier also makes faucets that set temperature based on facial recognition and wine coolers that alert owners when their vintage stock is running low.

Haier has mastered the art of coming up with new business strategies to keep wowing customers, in the present and in the future. It all starts with identifying future customer needs and then developing strategies to meet them—and to meet them in ways that thrill customers.

EMPOWERING TEAMS

A critical part of delighting customers, often overlooked, is the role that your employees play at all stages. We have said repeatedly that your employees are your most significant assets in understanding your customer needs and thrilling them. Your employees should play a significant part in assessing needs, coming up with strategies, implementing them, and bringing the new strategies to life as they interact with customers.

Most leaders pay lip service to the idea of empowering their teams, especially teams that serve customers directly. Yet most organizations neither trust their employees to do the right thing nor allow them to make mistakes. Few organizations give their employees decision-making authority.

But all employees interacting with customers should have the power to make decisions on the spot—the kinds of decisions that an owner of a small business could make. Employees should be not only allowed but also encouraged to address customer concerns, provide service, and show customers how to use products. Only employees who are empowered to make decisions—who are trusted and are allowed to make mistakes—can do these things and satisfy customers. Unless an organization's culture supports frontline employees, employee empowerment is a pipe dream and customer engagement is nonexistent.

No one knows this better than Disney. From the day Disneyland opened, it has been staffed by empowered teams trained to communicate well with customers. Sixty-odd years later, the teams still work without much supervision and are encouraged to solve customer problems, without even waiting to be asked to do so. When customers even appear to have issues, the team member on the spot has the company's encouragement to reach out and find creative solutions. Disney calls this being "assertively friendly." Team members also are trained in trying to make the customer experience more fun. They all know how to answer questions about most aspects of the park, even if they work in a different part of it. They pass out stickers, FastPasses, birthday pins, and free bags and shirts. Every team member at Disney Parks is trained to be an effective communicator.

Six Senses, named by the *Telegraph* the World's Best Hotel Group for 2015/2016, takes the Disney approach to a whole new level. Employees are trained in what the company calls "empathy." The Guest Experience Makers resolve customer issues on their own. They are encouraged to actively observe the guests' likes and dislikes and then to suggest to each guest ways to make staying at the resort more comfortable and enjoyable.

For example, I find snorkeling trying, due to my fear of depth. Our Guest Experience Maker learned about my difficulties and asked one of the resort's marine biologists to make a private trip with us so that I could snorkel without group pressure. The restaurant manager made a personal effort to offer us Sri Lankan food—not part of the dinner menu—and did this without telling management. This focus on customers through empowering the frontline team to make decisions on the spot, without management intervention, is unique and is much appreciated by all the guests. People from different parts of the world, and of all ages, rated their experience highly and wanted to come back.

Are you empowering your employees to that extent? You can achieve employee empowerment by taking the following steps.

Involve the current team in selecting and training new members.
Selecting team members your team can trust is the first step in empowering employees. Most companies' recruitment process judges applicants on their past performance, but the past is not a good predictor of how well someone can do a new job or fit in at a new company. It would be better to let the current team select new members. This has been shown to produce a team that can trust and depend on its members. It also gives the whole team a stake in and accountability for the new team member's performance, which is improved when the current team trains new members. At both Disney and Starbucks, the team on the spot trains new members, and these companies are consistently rated highly by their employees and their customers.

Develop a customer-focused, shared purpose. Teams who are all working toward a clearly defined common goal are happier, work better together, and thus can make customers happier. Walt Disney achieved this not only through training but also by calling those who work at Disneyland "cast members" and making it clear that they all are expected to put on the best show possible for customers. Starbucks not only calls its employees "partners" but also gives them stock options.

Create supportive leadership. Empowered teams feel that the managers have their backs and are open to new ideas from them. To empower teams, leaders have to let go of the steering wheel and allow people to make wrong decisions and then learn from them. At Haier, management's mandate is to support the frontline team. The company is significantly reducing the middle layer of management to speed up decision-making and allow teams to learn from their mistakes.

Give team members authority. Teams feel empowered when they have the power to make decisions on their own. For this to happen in a way that works for the company, employees need to be taught how to make the right choices for the customers. At Six Senses, team members are allowed to fix a problem, whatever it costs. Of course, costs are relevant, but the company emphasizes that the team members' first goal is to do right by the customers. Profits are not their responsibility.

Recognize success. Positive enforcement for good behavior both empowers teams and encourages them to focus on the company's priorities. Six Senses gives its employees bonuses for positive feedback from customers on social media. In addition, during weekly meetings, colleagues celebrate one another's achievements in making a customer's stay special.

Studies show that empowered teams deliver results even when they have poor to nonexistent leadership. We were not impressed with the Six Senses top leadership, as they made only minimal effort to engage with customers. But we were amazed by their operational lead and staff, which reflected positively on the leaders and their philosophy.

To take a dramatic example from history: In the eighteenth century, German commanders were allowed to give their subordinates a mission but were not allowed to tell them how to accomplish it. This was a tradition in the German military. During the Battle of Zorndorf, in 1758, the German general von Seydlitz refused direct orders from King Frederick to attack the Russians. As he said to the king's messenger, "Tell the king that, after the battle, my head is at his disposal, but that meanwhile I would make use of it." At an appropriate time, von Seydlitz charged the Russians and won the battle—and was subsequently congratulated by the king.

The same principle of empowering those who are actually doing the work applies to business. An empowered team can compensate for bad leadership. But good leadership can't achieve good results without an empowered team.

PAYING ATTENTION TO DETAIL

Customers love products or services that show attention to detail. Though Six Senses resorts aren't over-the-top luxurious, employees at every level are paying attention to every detail. The music played in a guest's bedroom, temperature, snacks, and lighting are all chosen to suit an individual guest's tastes. Even the bikes have individualized name-plates! Of course, guests noticed, and these details even became a topic for conversation at meals.

Similarly, visitors to Japan are usually impressed by the attention to detail everywhere, from the way purchases are perfectly wrapped to the beautiful arrangement of hotel breakfast trays. The Japanese attention to detail is legendary and is defined by two words: *omotenashi* and *kaizen*. *Omotenashi* means "The customer is always right," but many in Japan will translate it to "The customer is a god." For example, when planes take off, airport workers bow. When a customer enters or leaves a taxi, the driver always opens and closes the door. Even inexpensive purchases are wrapped with care to look beautiful. The list goes on and on in Japan; everyone who interacts with customers tries to provide the best service possible.

Kaizen means "continuous improvement." Every member of Japanese society is taught to pay attention to and continually improve upon the work they do. Once anyone figures out a better way, everyone else wholeheartedly adopts the new approach. It's a way of life in Japan, and it involves everyone from the CEO to the lowliest employee. It's no accident that Japan became an industrial powerhouse.

All great leaders and organizations pay attention to details. Walt Disney rode the rides in his park himself to ensure they provided the best experience for customers. And the tradition of paying attention to every detail at Disneyland continues, from the placement of trash cans to the food and service in the cafeteria; everything is continuously perfected for the best customer experience.

Steve Jobs, too, was famous for sweating the small stuff. He obsessed over everything, from the icons on the iPhone to the type of materials used in Apple retail stores to the lettering on the logo. He is rumored to have spent thirty minutes debating the shade of gray for the bathroom signs in Apple stores. That obsession with detail percolates down throughout the organization. People have debated and thought through every detail of Apple's products—whether it's the design of the Apple Pencil or the iOS flashlight icon. The box containing the first Macs even had a smiling face on the underside of the flap—something customers saw only for a second, when they first opened the box containing their new Mac. But those who noticed it were pleasantly surprised and smiled back.

Attention to detail starts at the top, and it can be encouraged and taught to everyone in the organization by following these steps.

Champion attention to detail. The attention to detail at Disney and Apple started with the founders' values. That is the only way attention to detail can start—from the top—but it can't end there. The entire organization has to strive for and insist on perfection, from the design of products or services through their delivery; in their day-to-day activities; and in every interaction with the public, whether online or on the phone or in person. Employees will come to feel proud of their performance and that of their company. The best way for leaders to achieve this throughout the organization is by example and positive reinforcement.

Develop good managers. Managers play an essential role in emphasizing attention to detail. They are the ones who ensure quality and discipline. They're like the centurions in the Roman army. Good Roman generals knew the value of centurions and selected them carefully. Centurions were responsible for training the troops, and they were on the front lines during battle. They led by example. A good centurion could keep his men fighting—and often could eventually win, even when his troops were outnumbered. Roman generals recognized this fact. Centurions not only were paid well but also received bonuses at the end of campaigns, based on how well their troops had fought. Similarly, today's leaders, like Roman generals choosing and rewarding centurions, should choose managers for their ability to develop talent and then reward them for the performance of those they manage.

Encourage employees to take pride in their work. Pride inspires people to take ownership of their work and achieve a level of perfection that everyone will recognize. Whether you are a janitor, a design engineer, or a financial analyst, pride in your work shows in the minutest of details. As a new consultant, I was asked to check every detail and every number that was presented to the client. Even a small error reflected poorly on the team in general, and on me. If errors happen often, people will not trust you and may not want you on their team. Moreover, pride is contagious. Once you get one team to achieve a higher standard, every other team will put in its best effort. Everyone in Japan takes pride in their work and in the smallest detail. If they do not, others notice.

Review and ask to redo. Someone should review the work of any new member so that he or she knows how to pay attention to detail and to do the assigned work well. This on-the-job training comes first; team empowerment comes later, once the employee is adequately trained to perform the job.

The person reviewing a trainee's work must provide useful feedback and ask the trainee to redo each task until the work reaches a realistic level of perfection. Having someone supervise and provide immediate constructive feedback on how to improve can be a great motivator and learning experience during training. It teaches you the details of the work and makes you understand what perfection looks like.

At many consulting firms, every new consultant has to spend hours with their managers to review and redo their work. It doesn't matter how late it is; no one goes home until the work has received the manager's approval. The same principle was true when Roman centurions taught their soldiers how to fight. Centurions set the example of what was acceptable for all their soldiers to follow. They lived and died together on the battlefield.

Recognize work well done. Money is not the sole motivator. Whenever anyone in the organization does something well, acknowledge and reward their progress. Provide rewards publicly, with certification, celebrations, and the like. Another way to reward individuals who do well is to give them opportunities for growth by giving them important assignments. That's a sure way of showing the whole organization the importance of attention to detail. Group recognition can do wonders in getting people to achieve organizational goals.

Culture determines any organization's values and norms, and if attention to detail is not part of the culture, an organization will ultimately fail. This is as true of countries as it is of companies. For example, despite all the progress made by India, Indians are not known for their attention to detail. The idea that it's not only okay but even sensible and polite to accept standards, conditions, and performance at work that people in other cultures would complain about is widespread in India. It has kept the peace in a largely poor society for centuries. But this attitude, which Indians call *chalta hai* (It's okay), has been detrimental to manufacturing.

Because of *chalta hai*—and the resulting lack of attention to detail—India still struggles to become a manufacturing powerhouse like China. People constantly take shortcuts. Prime Minister Modi's ambitious Make in India project, which asked multinationals to manufacture products in India for consumption within the country, has had only mixed success. The program was initially targeted at military hardware, but the Indian military kept finding that indigenously produced rifles offered subpar performance in field tests.[6] So now it has to import even basic items—because the culture does not value attention to detail.

BUSINESS REINVENTION

Great companies in any culture evolve, keeping their businesses relevant to changing customer needs by adopting the mind-set of continuous reinvention. Disney and Haier are great examples, but it's not surprising that there are few others, because visualizing future needs and developing strategies for them is difficult. You have to be willing to throw away strategies that aren't working now (no matter how well they have worked in the past) and to embrace new strategies. We've provided several strategies, but you have to be willing to discard them all and find new ones when any, including ours, no longer meet your customers' needs. Not surprisingly, most companies don't do this. Instead, they stick to what worked in the past, dig in, and blame customers.

The ability to evolve revolves around three simple things: visualizing future customer needs and developing strategies to meet those needs, empowering teams to thrill customers, and paying attention to detail. These sound simple. They're easy to say, but they are extremely difficult to do.

Most companies struggle to empower employees to thrill customers. Disney has been sharing its employee training secrets with all and sundry for decades. However, most other companies can't seem to get their teams oriented toward customers the way the Disney cast members are. This is because you can't get customer orientation just by telling your employees to do it, or even by training them to do it. You have to empower your teams to focus on customers, and at most companies that means a significant change in culture. It starts with employee selection and goes on to your ability to trust in employees to make the right decisions. This is not an easy task.

Many leaders say they want to delegate responsibility, but delegating responsibility means letting people fail sometimes, and most leaders can't tolerate failure in other people. Investors trust leaders to make decisions; leaders should extend the same trust to their employees. But that's a significant change in mind-set for most business cultures, driven as they are by top-down authority and decision-making.

Leaders have to change their mind-set in order to evolve with customers. They must become eager to change their strategies and embrace their employees' pivotal role in wowing customers. When leaders do that, customers will sing their praises—and their companies will prosper—for generations to come. Even two generations after Walt's death, Disney is the world's eighth most powerful brand and was number one on the *Forbes* 2018 list of the world's most highly regarded companies—because it has kept evolving.[7]

Conclusion
CHOOSING AND IMPLEMENTING THE STRATEGIES

W E'VE DESCRIBED THE DIFFERENT customer-focused strategies, but how do you choose and implement the ones that will work best for your company? Not all strategies are appropriate for every company. You have to select the ones that best address your customers' needs and then figure out how to get your organization to support and implement these strategies. This is not easy, as many of the changes entail a radical departure from current practices. Even when leaders understand the benefits a customer-focused strategy will bring to their business, many are still reluctant to change. They don't want to rock the boat during their short stay at the helm, so they cling to old strategies until customers disrupt their company—and sometimes even after that.

To see how this all plays out at an actual company, consider this true story. I received a call from the strategy officer of a leading facilities management company—let's call them FMP. They were about to lose their biggest client, a large New York bank that gave them half a billion dollars' worth of business each year. FMP maintained and managed the bank's offices, branches, warehousing, and other facilities. FMP took care of almost everything physical: cleaning, security, catering, moving people from one office to another, project management for office renovation, and much more. But the bank had grown increasingly frustrated with the job FMP was doing and, when the bank threatened to cancel the contract, FMP's strategy officer realized he had to do something. But what?

The bank had turned its facility management over to FMP, assuming that the cost of taking care of its spaces would thereby go down. The bank figured FMP would pay lower wages, for instance, thus reducing cost to the bank. But the charges kept going up every year. FMP did pay its people lower wages, but it charged the bank for every little thing its workers did, including extra costs for extra services. If, say, someone at the bank called FMP to get coffee grounds off the rug after a workday spill, FMP sent someone in immediately—and charged the bank heftily for the service.

The trouble began when the bank executives came under pressure to reduce costs. They changed the contract with FMP from a per-service fee to a fixed fee and stipulated that the fee must decrease by 5% to 10% each year. FMP signed the new contract but quickly realized that they were losing money—a lot of money. So FMP cut back on its services, not just in its response to calls from bank employees but also in regularly scheduled things. For example: FMP began cleaning bank branches only three times a week rather than the former five. These cost-cutting changes enraged the bank. It was at this point that the bank threatened to end the contract and FMP called us.

The first step in fixing the problem was to choose the right strategy, and for that, we needed to understand FMP's customers and their needs. This included *all* their customers, not just the bank. As it turned out, FMP was having the same kinds of troubles with all their customers. Without a new service model that met their customers' needs, fast, they would be disrupted. (Recall the lesson of chapter 5: customers won't wait.) After analyzing FMP's contracts with customers, we found that traditional contracts with a small portion of profit at risk represented only 45% of FMP's revenue (figure 27), and even that was decreasing. Contracts with a majority of profit at risk made up 40% of FMP's revenue, and the remaining 15% of revenue came from fixed-price contracts. Both the latter contract types were increasing in number.

To reduce costs, you have to understand what's driving them. As we analyzed FMP's costs, we realized that close to 85% of costs came

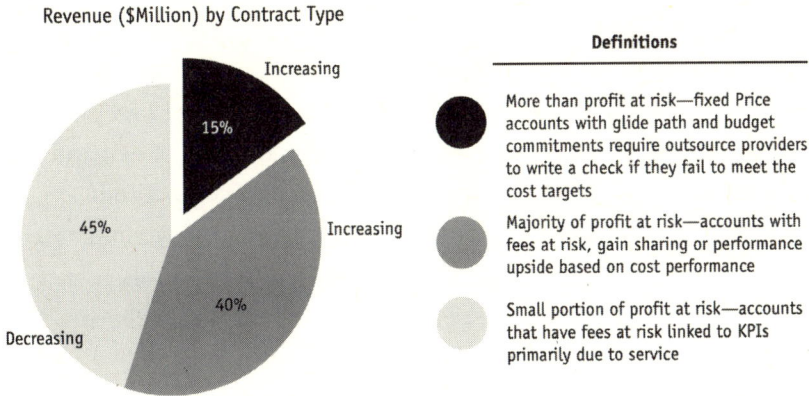

Revenue ($Million) by Contract Type

FIGURE 27 Changing customer requirements for outsourcing providers. Source: Three S Consulting.

from third-party providers such as janitorial services, security services, cafeteria operations, and the like. Further analysis revealed that these costs were driven by labor and that FMP had already aggressively negotiated the pricing. These providers were already paying their employees close to minimum wage and—not surprisingly, given that they were in New York City—were having retention problems. Wages couldn't be lowered any more, and in some cases they had to go up.

The only way to reduce costs was to get more work done in the allotted hours. If you've ever hired contractors, or just watched road crews, you know that they spend a lot of time standing around, waiting for material, for other crews, for equipment. Third-party-provider crews were also spending a lot of time waiting, as well as traveling from site to site. We realized that by reducing downtime, wait time, and travel time, FMP could significantly reduce costs. To do this effectively, FMP would have to schedule and optimize routes across customers. For example, in New York City, FMP had customers in the same high-rise as, or just across the street from, the bank. If they coordinated scheduled work so that service providers could quickly move from one customer to another, they would get more done during each shift.

We recommended that FMP give each provider handheld terminals, enabling FMP to guide providers from one work site to another, as Uber does with its drivers. Initially, this change would be a lot of work, but by making the change, FMP could meet the bank's demand for reduced costs *and* gain a significant advantage over competitors.

So far, so good. But after selecting a strategy, you have to implement it. This is almost always tricky, and so it proved to be in this case. The FMP leaders balked and refused to invest in the changes, believing that their customers had no choice. But that belief was wrong.

Fed up with FMP's poor service, high costs, and refusal to change, the bank began hiring its own people to manage the facilities. FMP's margins continued to go down, and their conflicts with customers continued to go up. Not surprisingly, organic revenue stopped growing. As of this writing, FMP is trying to save the situation with one of the outdated strategies we discussed in chapter 2: buying competitors. But it's only a matter of time before an upstart completely disrupts the industry with a new service model.

To get a sense of how skillful your company is at choosing and implementing customer-pleasing strategies, ask yourself these questions.

- What customer-focused strategies would be appropriate for your company? Why?
- How effective are leaders at implementing these strategies and empowering employees to do so?

If you are very effective at identifying and implementing customer-focused strategies, then your customers will help you disrupt the current providers. You are set up for growth and success. If you are not, you have to identify and implement customer-focused strategies quickly. Otherwise, customers will disrupt you.

SELECTING THE RIGHT CUSTOMER-FOCUSED STRATEGIES

This book details five primary customer-focused strategies: service, personalization, speed, quality, and reinvention. As the FMP example shows, sometimes a portion of a strategy—in FMP's case, changing the service model, as discussed in chapter 5—is all you need. To identify what's appropriate for your business, begin with customer needs, then find unique ways to address those needs. What will work for one company may not work for others. It all depends on what you're offering and the customer segments you're targeting. For example, in the apparel industry, Zozotown, the Japanese retailer, wins through personalization (chapter 4), whereas Zara wins through speed (chapter 5). They're targeting different segments. Sometimes a combination of strategies works as well. Amazon employs both service (chapter 3) and speed (chapter 5) to address their customers' needs.

Table 3 highlights the kinds of strategies that companies in different industries typically use now, and those that would be more

TABLE 3

Potential Customer-Focused Strategies by Industry

INDUSTRY	CUSTOMER NEEDS	CURRENT DOMINANT STRATEGIES	POTENTIAL CUSTOMER FOCUSED STRATEGIES
Pharmaceuticals	Drugs • Prevent • Cure • Affordable	• Incremental innovation • Mass manufacturing • Lobbying	• Personalization (chapter 4) • Quality (chapter 6) • Speed (chapter 5)
Apparel Retail	Products/clothing • Fit • Fabric • Fashion • Affordable	• Jazzy storefront • Branding • Mass manufacturing	• Service (chapter 3) • Personalization (chapter 4) • Speed (chapter 5)
Automotive	Transportation • Fast • Affordable • Safe • Low Pollution	• Incremental innovation • Branding • Mass manufacturing • Globalization	• Customization (chapter 4) • Service (chapter 3) • Quality (chapter 6)
Consumer Goods	Products • Healthy / Natural • Affordable	• Incremental innovation • Branding • Mass manufacturing • Globalization	• Quality (chapter 6) • Personalization (chapter 4) • Speed (chapter 5)

Source: Three S Consulting.

appropriate. Note that these are not rules, just what is most likely to work in a given industry. Other strategies from the book may work just as well, if not better. The important thing is to choose based on customer needs and segments.

To show how companies in different industries might choose their strategies, let us start with table 3 which summarizes customer needs, current dominant strategies, and new strategies for a few industries.

Pharmaceuticals

Customers want to be healthy and are looking for affordable prevention and cures. They desire a healthy life. Three strategies could deliver on those needs: personalization (chapter 4), quality (chapter 6), and speed (chapter 5). For some segments, a combination would work best.

- *Personalization* in medicine can be based on genetics or on patient history and prognosis. The industry has already discussed using genetics quite extensively; other ways of personalizing medicine haven't been talked about as much. Most medicines are prescribed based on the patient's illness, but many are overprescribed or inappropriate. A study by the *Telegraph* in the United Kingdom states that millions of people take a statin (cholesterol medication) needlessly.[1] And even when the medicine is appropriate for the patient, dosages tend to be standardized. Finding the right dosage and combination of drugs based on an individual's medical history, speed of recovery, or reaction to the medicine could be a game changer. More personalization has huge potential benefits for patients, such as bringing them quickly back to health, avoiding complications, and preventing future disease.

- *Quality* continues to be an important factor for the pharmaceutical and medical devices industries (remember MediDevi). Some pharmaceutical companies can use quality to better address customer needs, particularly in developing countries, where tampering with authentic products and selling spurious ones continue to harm customers.

- *Speed* is crucial in this industry because, even in developed countries, too many drugs are sold close to their expiration date. Getting products from the manufacturing site to patients quickly, without holding inventory, could improve the efficacy of products and public health. For example, flu vaccines may be ineffective because companies have to develop vaccines long before anyone knows what strain of the virus will prevail in that season. If pharmaceutical companies could speed up their vaccine creation process and supply chains, they could respond to flu viruses faster, which could save lives. Speed is also important for products that are focused more on prevention, such as vitamins and herbs, and for personalized medications.

Affordability is key to long-term survival in this industry. Look at what happened to Mylan and its EpiPens. The pens cost less than $2 to produce, and Mylan sold them for $57 in 2007. Then, in 2016, it raised the price to $700. The public outcry resulted in congressional hearings and the introduction of generics. But Mylan is not alone. These aggressive pricing practices are all too common, and in the long run they don't work; customers turn against companies they see as price gougers. This trend will grow, as millennials demand ethical and transparent practices and won't buy from companies that don't adopt them.

Apparel Retail

Customer needs in the apparel industry are fit, fabric, fashion, speed, and affordability. This industry has been more affected by millennials than others. Strategies such as service (chapter 3), personalization (chapter 4), and speed (chapter 5), alone or in combination, can help retailers address customer needs, depending on the company's offering and targeted customer segment. Whatever strategy is being adopted, a company's offerings need to be affordable or millennials won't buy them.

- *Service* is the easiest way to get customers to spend more. Realizing this, many more companies now offer home delivery. Many companies will need to weigh the advantages of brick and mortar versus online stores and look at how to deliver great service in each—or using both. For example, a retailer might offer style advice in its physical store whereas managing orders could take place online, for easy tracking of user information and provision of future recommendations.

- Affordable *personalization* is a huge opportunity for apparel retailers. If you are selling custom-made clothes, such as suits and shoes, and can do this affordably for customers, you'll have a huge advantage.

- *Speed* continues to be important if you are selling a commodity or anything standardized. Long lead times and product unavailability could cost you customers. Finding a way to address your impatient customer needs quickly is critical.

Additionally, the industry needs to stop making returns difficult and alienating customers in other ways, such as by banning those who return too often. And because millennials are socially and environmentally conscious, counting on customers to throw away their old clothes and buy new ones is a doomed strategy. The industry will need to use other strategies to grow demand.

Automotive

Customers are looking for fast, affordable, and safe transportation that doesn't pollute the environment. Customization (chapter 4), service (chapter 3), and quality (chapter 6), alone or in combination, are all strategies that can deliver on these goals and attract customers.

- *Personalization* may not be practical in the near future, but automotive companies can customize their offerings by customer segment to make them affordable. For example, city drivers need easy-to-park cars, while rural drivers need good shock absorbers and four-wheel drive. Selling cars with both sets of features will add little value from most customers' perspective, but it will increase costs. Similarly, cars designed for developing countries need to be affordable and reliable on bad roads, but amenities like sunroofs are probably unnecessary if they add to the car's cost.

  Cars explicitly designed for ride-hailing needs should offer affordability, comfortable rides, easy cleaning, a good music system, and reliability. Amenities like assisted driving or parking or a sunroof may not be of value for ride-hailing customers.

  In short, car manufacturers can create products that cater to the different needs of their different segments without increasing costs—if they pay attention to what each segment actually needs.

- *Service* will become important, as the repeat customer rate is absymal.[2] The industry has to figure out how to retain current customers by changing the whole buying experience, servicing cars better, and disposing of them responsibly. Tesla is already experimenting with delivering cars, and even repair personnel, to customers' doors. But most of the industry is stuck in the 1980s and needs a complete overhaul.

- *Quality* will remain crucial. Servicing cost and frequent recalls not only add costs but also create customer credibility issues.

The big issue the industry should be focusing on is affordability. New cars are beyond the means of younger people, and older cars are too expensive to maintain.[3] Finding ways to reduce both the purchase price and the lifetime cost of vehicles will address customer needs and increase the industry's longevity.

Consumer Goods

Millennials are looking for healthy natural products. Quality (chapter 6), personalization (chapter 4), and speed (chapter 5) can help the industry become more customer focused.

- *Quality* of products and ethical sourcing of raw materials will become increasingly important because millennials are so socially and environmentally conscious. Companies will benefit by developing healthy, environmentally friendly products from natural materials. However, because boomers will continue to buy the brands they trust, companies should not be in a hurry to get rid of their current brands. The transition from the old to the new can be made as customer demand changes.

- Companies will benefit from *personalization* based on customer preferences, preferred ingredients in different geographies, and affordability. A database with customer preferences would undoubtedly help companies personalize their products and address the needs of different segments.

- *Speed* remains critical when launching new products or meeting changing customer needs. Millennials are impatient and have low brand loyalty. Companies that meet their changing needs quickly will be the winners.

Finally, big companies may benefit by forming alliances with regional companies. For example, if Patanjali products become successful with millennials in the United States, an alliance between Patanjali and a Western multinational could be beneficial to both. Customer-focused strategies have to be tailored for each company based on the segments they support, even for companies within the same industry.

For example, strategies that would work for Procter & Gamble may not work for Unilever. Choosing and implementing the right strategy requires careful work.

However, all companies that count on old strategies that don't work, such as incremental innovation, need to start choosing new strategies based on customer needs. Doing this—and developing operations to support them—will make companies and their products more relevant to customers and will provide long-term investor value, if the new strategies have organizational support. Having a plan for getting an organization to support the new strategy is crucial. Communication alone cannot make it happen, because the strategies discussed here will be such a radical change that they will require a new organizational perspective and many systemic changes.

CHANGING ORGANIZATION PERSPECTIVE

A company is like a large ship—changing direction requires cooperation from everyone, not just the captain. When it comes to implementing new strategies, organizational changes are key, and these require systematic, sequential planning. Here are the main steps.

Step 1: Change Incentives

Most companies use stocks and stock options based on financial performance as the main form of compensation for their leaders. This has to change. Instead, leaders should be rewarded for how well they deliver on customer needs. Investors should encourage the leadership team to think more like long-term owners and less in terms of three- to five-year assignments. Having customer metrics determine CEO and leadership compensation would help, too. These metrics should be diversified to include such things as customer satisfaction ratings, customer retention rates, and growth of the customer base. Surveys performed by third parties and feedback on social media both should be used. Once incentives for leaders have been fixed, it should be rolled out to the rest of the organization.

Step 2: Organize in Customer-Facing Groups

Most companies are organized functionally, into silos such as sales, marketing, manufacturing, and finance. The idea is that these areas are so different that employees should specialize in them. But this thinking is a leftover from the industrial age. Specialization played a more significant role then than it does today. These days, what counts is responding to customer needs in an entrepreneurial way, as companies like Haier have. Their customer-facing organization has radically improved the company's connection to customer needs, and other companies need to do this too or be left behind.

Customers don't care whether your employees are from marketing or IT or somewhere in the supply chain. All they care about is how well you meet their needs. Functional silos work against meeting customer needs; employees tend to feel more loyalty to the department or function than to the customers. This is inevitable when employee compensation and promotions are driven by how happy the employees keep their boss. Over time, this leads to leaders and middle managers who are all completely disconnected from customers. When companies try to work around this with a matrix organization (in which employees report to a functional boss and a business boss), the result is usually greater confusion and slower decision-making. Lack of customer focus remains the same. Haier has experimented with customer-facing teams with great success.

To achieve customer focus, create teams organized around customer segments rather than geographic location, type of product, or size. Empower these teams and build support for them into the organization. These customer-facing groups could each consist of people in sales, research and development, marketing, finance, and operations. The exact mix will depend upon the kind of customer the group supports, but each should have responsibility for revenue and profit and loss, along with the flexibility to link to customers' longer-term priorities. This is more entrepreneurial than most big corporations today are.

Chapter 3 provided detail on creating customer segments, but one warning here: When companies organize around customer segments, many tend to lose focus on operations. This, and the organization's increasing complexity, can overwhelm an organization. FMP, for example, was organized in customer-facing teams, but their operations and their management of third-party providers didn't support those teams well. The organizations supporting customer teams must excel in their areas of expertise and act strategically. The objective of the support teams should be to develop leading platforms, manage risk, share knowledge, and provide oversight. To achieve this, support organizations should be encouraged to compete with other providers in the market. They should be allowed to sell their services to other companies or directly to customers.

In short, the entrepreneurial spirit should be encouraged throughout the organization—not just in the customer-facing teams.

Step 3: Develop a Customercentric Culture

It's fashionable to talk about a company's culture, and many companies try to create cultures that make them unique among the competition. However, most go about it the wrong way, focusing on things like free food, open offices, parties, employee trips, open presentations by high-level executives, and gyms. None of these things focus employees on customers or encourage attention to detail. Companies that historically have done well and continue to do well, companies like Southwest and Disney, have created and continue to support truly customercentric cultures. They make their mission clear to everyone, as in the following.

- According to Amazon's jobs website, "When Amazon launched in 1995, it was with the mission 'to be Earth's most customer-centric company, where customers can find and discover anything they might want to buy online, and [it] endeavors to offer its customers the lowest possible prices.'"[4]

- Southwest's website says, "We like to think of ourselves as a Customer Service company that happens to fly airplanes (on schedule, with personality and perks along the way)."[5]

- Apple's employee training manual states, "Your job is to understand all of your customers' needs—some of which they may not even realize they have."[6]

- Disney cast members are taught "The guest isn't always right, but let them be wrong with dignity."

These companies don't just talk the talk, they walk the walk. Their customers know it and love them. Not surprisingly, all are leaders in their industries, both in customer satisfaction and in revenue/profit growth.

As we have seen, attention to detail and continuous improvement are vital parts of these companies' cultures; you can't have a truly customer-focused culture without them. Only when every employee is encouraged to improve their work processes and deliver value to customers will you succeed. This means that everyone in the company tries every day not only to improve their own work processes but also to share with others what they've learned—including what they learn from customer feedback. Companies that do this continually improve and achieve *omotenashi*—delighting customers in every way.

Step 4: Focus on Employee Development

Employees are assets, and companies that succeed invest in them. Happy employees lead to better customer interactions. So recruit them carefully, pay them fairly, reward them appropriately, train them well, allow them to make decisions without fear, and let them fail safely.

The recruiting process should focus on hiring employees who are customer oriented. This is particularly true for customer-facing teams. Consider how Southwest does it. In addition to employees' ability to perform their respective job well—that is, the pilot should be able to fly planes safely—the company also looks for three attributes in a candidate:

- A warrior spirit, or the desire to excel, act with courage, persevere, and innovate.

- A servant's heart, or the ability to put others first, treat everyone with respect, and proactively serve customers.

- A fun-loving attitude, including passion, joy, and an aversion to taking oneself too seriously.[7]

Every candidate is rated across these attributes to assess whether they will fit with Southwest's culture, irrespective of the position for which they are being hired. Even promotions are tied to these traits. People are measured both by results *and* by how they achieved the results. In a 2014 employee survey, 86% of employees said they were proud to work for Southwest. Carefully defining the traits you need in employees to keep customers happy usually results in happy employees, too.

Once you have hired the right person, the next step is onboarding and training to help them get oriented toward customers. Consider how the Disney resorts does it. A new employee spends a full six weeks in training, during which time they learn that they are not selling a product, they are selling an experience. Only when they have imbibed this do employees even meet guests.

Most customer-focused strategies fail because the organization is not oriented toward customers. Pushing an organization to change its focus through brute force or a leader's charisma may work for a year or two, but without structural change, directional changes don't last. The organization goes back to its old ways once the leader leaves. But changes are possible. Disney and Haier show that even large corporations can reinvent themselves—through committed leadership and radical structural change.

SOCIETAL IMPLICATIONS

People think failing businesses do not affect a country's economy and wealth. They are wrong. Businesses play a critical role in any society's employment and prosperity. Now we are at an inflection point—the failure of companies to become customer focused can affect not only the companies themselves but also a whole country.

Consider Finland. In the early 2000s, its industries and high standard of living placed this small country among the world's top twenty nations. Finland doesn't have oil, but its vast forests and paper exports were big business—and it became a technology hub, too. Nokia contributed 4% to Finland's gross domestic product in 2000. But then Apple launched the iPhone, and Nokia failed. Its phones didn't address customer needs for internet connectivity on the go. Then the iPad lowered paper consumption as more and more customers read news and magazines on tablets. Since the 2008 recession, Finland's economy has lagged behind that of the United States and all the EU countries except Italy.[8]

Other countries are in the same situation. Solar energy will eventually disrupt oil- and gas-producing countries. Venezuela's economy is already reeling due to a drop in oil prices. When the consumption of carbon-based fuels drops, as it probably will within a few years, Middle Eastern countries' economies will drop with them. So will the economies of Russia, Norway, the United Kingdom, and Denmark, unless they find other growth drivers for their economies.

The U.S. economy will be disrupted, too, unless corporations make radical changes. American corporations are so disconnected from their customers that they are losing to upstarts in all parts of the world, and at home, too. The largest companies, like Walmart, ExxonMobil, GE, AT&T, and even Apple, are not growing their revenues and profits organically. Most Americans assume that disrupters will be another American company, so that, at a national level, the money and jobs will flow from one set of companies to another. They point to U.S. leadership in technology and innovation and say that American corporations will continue to succeed.

This confidence is frightening and is not justified by reality. American car companies lost to Japanese car companies in the 1980s because of their failure to deliver the quality that customers wanted, not because American companies were not innovating. Today, competitors are coming from all parts of the world. Chinese and Indian companies are connecting better with customer needs and will eventually surpass their American counterparts. In household appliances, smartphones, solar energy, and mobile payments, Chinese companies are already beating their American counterparts.

There is a dire need for American companies to make radical changes, not just for their own growth and survival but also for the health of the American economy. Otherwise, the prosperity the United

States has enjoyed for so long will end. The money and talent will go to other countries—countries whose companies create value for their customers. Darwin's laws of natural selection are as valid in the global economy as they are in the animal kingdom. The key to survival in this era of changing global customer needs is to focus on those needs and then adapt—faster and better than the competition. It's not too late for U.S. companies, but they must change their focus and adopt new strategies—*now*.

APPENDIX

DISRUPTION ASSESSMENT

ANSWERING THE QUESTIONS IN this assessment will help you to evaluate a company's potential for disruption and the opportunities in its industry, and then to identify how the company could become more customer focused.

The assessment can be used for several different purposes. If you're a start-up hoping to disrupt a market, it will reveal opportunities. If you're a leader at an established company, it will help you to identify new, more effective strategies. If you're looking for a job, it will help you to evaluate employers for their growth potential. Finally, if you're an investor, it will help you to identify companies that could become market leaders.

Whatever your purpose in taking the assessment, the more sources you use to come up with and validate your answers, the more accurate your perspective on the company (here, called AnyCo) will be.

POTENTIAL FOR DISRUPTION

The best way to identify the potential for disruption is to evaluate how customer focused a company is.

1. What customer needs is AnyCo addressing? Not addressing?
2. How well do AnyCo's products or services address customer needs?

   What other ways could AnyCo meet customer needs?

   How unique to each segment and market are AnyCo's offerings?

What are customers complaining about?

How is AnyCo's leadership addressing those complaints?

3. How effective is AnyCo in selling to both baby boomers and millennials?

How different are the needs of millennials from those of baby boomers, with regard to AnyCo's products and services?

How successful is AnyCo in selling to millennials?

4. Were AnyCo's innovations and technologies developed to meet specific customer needs or were they developed for technology's sake?

How well do AnyCo's innovation and technology strategies address customer needs?

What needs are not being addressed?

How could AnyCo meet these needs, with or without technology?

CURRENT BUSINESS STRATEGY EFFECTIVENESS

Once a company understands customer needs, it must deliver on them. Long-term business success depends on using the right strategies.

1. What are AnyCo's current strategies? How customer focused are these strategies?

2. How are customers reacting to the strategies?

3. What does customer feedback/reaction reveal about long-term risks?

4. What benefits would more customer-focused strategies bring to AnyCo?

GROWTH FROM CURRENT CUSTOMERS

Getting existing customers to spend more and do it profitably is the holy grail of business. Any company that is good at this will be a winner.

1. How much more or less are AnyCo's existing customers (or customer segments) spending now than they did a year ago? Two years ago?

    If they are not spending more, why?

2. What programs is AnyCo using to get customers to spend more?

    How effective are these programs in generating additional revenue?

3. What was the impact on margins for each of those programs?

    What has been the trend in profitability?

    What led to an increase or decrease in AnyCo's profitability?

4. How quickly are competitors catching up with AnyCo's strategies? What variations are they using to grow revenue from their existing customers?

AFFORDABLE PERSONALIZATION

As millennials become the dominant buying group from 2020 to 2025, demand for personalized products and services will increase. Companies that make personalization affordable will be the most successful, and the stickier those services are, the more successful they will be.

1. How adept is AnyCo at addressing customer needs rather than merely selling products or services?

2. How personalized are AnyCo's products or services?

    How well does AnyCo tailor its products or services to each customer?

    How are the customers responding to AnyCo's personalized services?

3. How affordable are AnyCo's personalized offerings?

    How well are AnyCo's operations set up to deliver person-
    alized offerings (tailored for each individual) rather than
    merely producing standard products or services?

    What challenges does AnyCo face in changing its operations
    to make personalization affordable?

RESPONDING QUICKLY TO CUSTOMER NEEDS

We live in an era of instant gratification. Whether they're buying a car
or a custom-made suit, customers want it their way, now. And if you
can't deliver it fast enough, they'll buy it from someone who can.

1. How quickly does AnyCo notice and respond to changing
    customer needs?

    How effective is AnyCo in noticing a change in customer
    needs?

    How long does AnyCo make customers wait before
    responding to changing needs? Why does it take so long?

    What has been AnyCo customers' reaction to the wait?

2. How long does AnyCo take to develop new products or services,
    bring them to market, and create effective service models?

    How quickly can AnyCo develop new products or services
    and bring them to market?

    How are customers reacting?

    How well does AnyCo change the service model to respond
    to changing customer needs?

3. How quickly are other companies in AnyCo's industry doing
    these things?

Are there other companies that are responding faster?

How are they able to respond to customer needs quickly?

What has been the reaction from customers?

BREAKTHROUGH QUALITY

More and more customers are reading peer reviews on Amazon and other sites before buying products or services. They're looking at product performance, service, and quality issues, and they believe what their peers tell them, not companies' claims or advertising. In this environment, all products and services are judged on their merit, according to how well they work for customers. Improving quality is a sure way of getting repeat business and attracting new customers with favorable reviews.

1. How do customers view the quality of AnyCo's products and services?

    How do customers review AnyCo's products and services? How do these reviews compare with reviews of competitors' products or services?

    What aspects of AnyCo do customers rave or complain about on social media? How has AnyCo responded to this feedback?

2. How much importance does AnyCo's leadership attach to quality?

    Does AnyCo leadership view quality as a game changer or more of a placeholder?

    How frequently does AnyCo leadership speak to customers and review customer quality feedback?

    What strategies is AnyCo developing to achieve quality leadership with customers?

3. How hard do AnyCo's internal organizations try to improve quality and delight customers?

> Where does quality rank among strategies used by AnyCo?

> What type of resources are devoted to a breakthrough in quality?

> How involved in quality improvement programs are AnyCo's customers and suppliers?

> How does AnyCo incentivize its operations team? Do these incentives support quality improvements?

REINVENTION

You may be very successful today, but if you fail to reinvent yourself as customer needs change, you will fail. It's hard to predict the future in anything, especially when it comes to customers who keep changing what they want. The only way to do it is to become skilled at creating strategies that support your customers' needs—and then to keep updating those strategies. You can only do that if your whole organization is set up to identify and respond to customers' needs as, and even before, they arise.

1. How does AnyCo plan to delight future customers?

> How does AnyCo identify future customer needs? What roles do customers, suppliers, and outside stakeholders play in the process?

> What strategies will help AnyCo meet future customer needs?

2. What organizational capability does AnyCo have to identify and respond to future needs?

> How does AnyCo leadership empower its team? What has been the team's feedback on empowerment? What are AnyCo's plans for increasing empowerment?

How does AnyCo instill attention to detail throughout its organization? How do leadership and managers champion attention to detail and train staff?

IMPLEMENTING CUSTOMER-FOCUSED STRATEGIES

Not all strategies are appropriate for every company. Leaders have to select the one that best addresses their customers' needs, then figure out how to get their organization to support and implement it.

1. What customer-focused strategies would be appropriate for AnyCo?

   What are the customer needs from the industry? What needs should AnyCo focus on addressing? Why?

   What customer strategies could help AnyCo address customer needs better? Why?

2. How will AnyCo implement these strategies?

   How capable and willing are leaders when it comes to implementing new strategies? What incentives are required to align leadership with the new strategies?

   How should the organization be structured and what type of culture is needed for the future? What employee development programs required reorienting the organization?

NOTES

INTRODUCTION

1. Dr. Rana Mehta et al., *Ayurveda 2.0: On the Cusp of Change* (Kerala: Confederation of Indian Industry and Price WaterhouseCoopers, November 2018), https://goo.gl/zs7Azo; ET Bureau, "Patanjali Plans to Overtake HUL by Next Year, Not Weighing IPO," *Economic Times*, January 17, 2018, https://goo.gl/bPM12M.

2. Campaign India Team, "Goafest 2017: Patanjali, India's Popular Ayurveda Brand to Take the World by Storm," *Campaign India*, April 6, 2017, https://goo.gl/11zTzJ.

3. Masoom Gupte, "HUL CEO Sanjiv Mehta Lists Four Easy Ways to Crack Innovation," *Economic Times of India*, January 9, 2017, https://goo.gl/geJnEi; TRA Research, "The Brand Trust Report 2017 Rankings," https://goo.gl/VCm7id.

4. Jamshid Vayghan, "Doing the Right Thing and Doing It the Right Way," *Forbes*, February 21, 2018, https://goo.gl/6Z6TyE.

CHAPTER 1 Customers Drive Disruption

1. "Japan's Start Today Gives Clothes Retailers a Glimpse of the Future," *Economist*, August 18, 2018, https://goo.gl/1C5Rdj.

2. Jay Yarow, "The Best Steve Jobs Quotes from His Biography," *Business Insider*, October 26, 2011, https://goo.gl/qEc1Jr.

3. Stephen Silver, "The Story of the Original iPhone, That Nobody Thought Was Possible," appleinsider, June 29, 2018, https://goo.gl/bpHKGX.

4. Jenni Marsh, "The Chinese Phone Giant that Beat Apple to Africa" *CNN Business*, October 10, 2018, https://goo.gl/cXue5f.

5. Meng Jing, "How Chinese Smartphone Makers Compete with Samsung and Apple in Overseas Markets," *South China Morning Post*, August 1, 2017, https://goo.gl/bYiZYK; Newley Purnell and Tripp Mickle, " 'It's Been a Rout': Apple's iPhones Fall Flat in World's Largest Untapped Market," *Wall Street Journal*, December 18, 2018, https://goo.gl/Z2qRjf; C. Scott Brown, "Xiaomi's Market Share Explodes in Europe," *Android Authority*, May 11, 2018, https://goo.gl/BCnCuX.

6. Arjun Kharpal, "Chinese Smartphone Makers Are Pushing into the U.S. Despite Huawei's Struggles," CNBC, March 1, 2018, https://goo.gl/Q5zGfV.

7. Paul Davidson, "The Economy Is Still All About—Who Else?—Boomers," *USA Today*, July 17, 2017, https://goo.gl/xSFYF7.

8. Don Peppers, "How 3M Lost (and Found) its Innovation Mojo," *Inc.*, May 9, 2016, https://goo.gl/yMNXgA.

9. Savanna Swain-Wilson, "10 Ways Gen Zs Spend Money Differently Than Their Gen X Parents," *Insider*, November 28, 2018, https://goo.gl/dWYXao.

10. Goldman Sachs, "Millennials Coming of Age," https://goo.gl/vM5vtG.

11. Graham Rapier, "Millennials' Coffee Preferences Are Wildly Different from Their Parents'—and Starbucks Is Set to Reap the Rewards," *Business Insider*, October 30, 2017, https://goo.gl/LVcgxF.

12. WebMD Health Services, "The Millennial Mindset: Health, Wellness and Control," WebMD, March 8, 2016, https://goo.gl/8q4VY7; Joshua D. Detre, Tyler B. Mark, and Benjamin M. Clark, "Understanding Why College-Educated Millennials Shop at Farmers Markets: An Analysis of Students at Louisiana State University," *Journal of Food Distribution Research* 41, no. 3 (November 2010), https://goo.gl/EMqNc4.

13. Julian Ryall, "Japan's Millennial Men Don't Drink, Don't Drive, Don't Worship Work—What Do They Do?," *South China Morning Post*, February 4, 2017, https://goo.gl/zaiDFt.

14. Time Video, "How Generation Z Will Change the World," *Time*, April 23, 2018, https://goo.gl/wciVmF.

15. Josh Mcallister, "The Future of the Workforce: What You Should Know About Generation Z," *HR Tech Weekly*, November 29, 2018, https://goo.gl/UDgWru.

16. Jamal Carnette, "Here's Why Investors Should Pay Attention to Campbell Soup's Struggles," *Motley Fool*, June 10, 2018, https://goo.gl/63iq5R.

17. Edmund Andrews, "Is Tech Disruption Good for the Economy?," Stanford Graduate School of Business, January 23, 2017, https://goo.gl/DR4x1n.

18. Hans Greimel and Naoto Okamura, "Japan Recruits Subaru, Uber and Boeing to Get Flying Cars Off the Ground," *Automotive News*, September 8, 2018, https://goo.gl/P1gWYP.

19. Richard Windsor, "If Waymo Is Having Difficulty, Everyone Else Must Be in a Right Autonomous Driving Pickle," *Forbes*, November 28, 2018, https://goo.gl/416JF2; David Biello, "Electric Cars Are Not Necessarily Clean," *Scientific America*, May 11, 2016, https://goo.gl/CWLD7k.

20. American Customer Satisfaction Index, "Publix vs. Trader Joe's, Costco vs. BJ's, Target vs. Walmart: ACSI Scores Show Which Retailers Customers Prefer," February 27, 2018, https://goo.gl/AtHXnM.

CHAPTER 2 Customer-Focused Strategies Needed to Avoid Disruption

1. William D. Cohan, "When Blue Chip Companies Pile on Debt, It's Time to Worry," *New York Times*, November 26, 2018, https://goo.gl/M4VGFA.

2. "Policies and Practices," Procter & Gamble, https://goo.gl/AwsM3U.

3. Sharon Terlep and Allison Prang, "P&G, After Slight Sales Gain, Puzzled by Weak U.S. Consumer Spending," *Wall Street Journal*, October 20, 2017, https://goo.gl/udEQmk.

4. Trian Partners, "Revitalize P&G Together: Vote the White Proxy Card," Trian Fund Management, September 6, 2017, https://goo.gl/5hRa8J

5. Carola Frydman and Dirk Jenter, "CEO Compensation," *Annual Review of Financial Economics* 2, no. 1 (December 2010): 75–102. Available at https://goo.gl/y9KU72.

6. Sean O'Kane, "Elon Musk's New $2.6 Billion Compensation Plan Approved by Tesla Shareholders," *The Verge*, March 21, 2018, https://goo.gl/K2rtJi; Matthew DeBord, "Elon Musk Didn't Used to Care About Short Sellers—Here's Why He Does Now," *Business Insider*, August 17, 2018, https://goo.gl/FvtLRB.

7. Matt Egan, "Corporate America Gives Out a Record $1 Trillion in Stock Buybacks," *CNN Business*, December 17, 2018, https://goo.gl/F8oZ4k.

8. Oriana Bandiera et al., "A Survey of How 1,000 CEOs Spend Their Day Reveals What Makes Leaders Successful," *Harvard Business Review*, October 12, 2017, https://goo.gl/zyJhwR; Jeff Cox, "Read GE's Full Turnaround Plan Here," CNBC, November 13, 2017, https://goo.gl/P2Uzun.

9. Sharon Terlep, "Rather Than Add More Blades to Its Razors, Gillette Trims Prices," *Wall Street Journal*, November 29, 2017, https://goo.gl/8wFtSv.

10. Arjun Kharpal, "Samsung Is Packing More Tech into Its Mid-Priced Smartphones to Appeal to Millennials," CNBC, September 3, 2018, https://goo.gl/6V23xa.

11. Dan Schawbel, "10 New Findings About the Millennial Consumer," *Forbes*, January 20, 2015, https://goo.gl/ZELjy8; David Kirkpatrick, "Study: 78% of Millennials Aren't Influenced by Celebrity Endorsements," *Marketing Dive*, December 4, 2017, https://goo.gl/iwkjmA.

12. Marie-Josee Cougard, "Chewing Gum Victim of Smartphones," *Les Echos*, June 25, 2017, https://goo.gl/jNDiUA; Mary Pflum, "Soon You'll Be Able to Check Out at Walmart Without Going to the Register," NBC, October 30, 2018, https://goo.gl/1LqPSB.

13. Neil Howe, "Are Millennials Killing Name Brands?," *Forbes*, November 20, 2018, https://goo.gl/moqq9X

14. Nick Kostov and Suzanne Vranica, "Turmoil on Madison Avenue as Marketers Push for Change," *Wall Street Journal*, March 1, 2018, https://goo.gl/uoFRgC; Lucy Handley, "Chief Marketers Have 'Significant Fear' About Ad Fraud—and Here's What Media Agencies Need to Do About It," CNBC, September 26, 2017, https://goo.gl/FCx539.

15. Brian Pascus, "The World's 3 Biggest Airlines Have All Raised Their Checked Baggage Fees," *Business Insider*, September 20, 2018, https://goo.gl/WP471V; Brian Sumers, "Congress Warns 5 Airline Execs They Must Improve Customer Service," Skift, May 2, 2017, https://goo.gl/dPV3Jb.

16. "The Retreat of the Global Company," *Economist*, January 28, 2017, https://goo.gl/1fXbkL

17. OpenSecrets.org, "Top Industries," Center for Responsive Politics, https://goo.gl/aPrWru. Accessed February 15, 2019.

18. Derek Thompson, "How Did Greek Yogurt Get So Popular?," *Atlantic*, August 23, 2011, https://goo.gl/8NUS9u.

19. Megan Durisin, "Chobani CEO: Our Success Has Nothing To Do With Yogurt," *Business Insider*, May 3, 2013, https://goo.gl/9zXpTH.

20. Steve Tobak, "Why Getting Fired Can Be the Best Thing For You," CBS News, July 28, 2011, https://goo.gl/A513b3.

CHAPTER 3   Customer-Focus Strategy 1: Win with Current Customers before Chasing after New Ones

1. Amy Gallo, "The Value of Keeping the Right Customers," *Harvard Business Review*, October 29, 2014, https://goo.gl/rkxjSR.

2. Panos Mourdoukoutas, "Walmart Needs to Reconnect with Customers and Employees," *Forbes*, February 18, 2016, https://goo.gl/4KahVS.

3. Gallo, "The Value of Keeping the Right Customers"; Fred Reichheld, "Prescription for Cutting Costs," Bain & Company, https://goo.gl/WzkGmD.

4. Heather Haddon and Laura Stevens, "Attention, Amazon Prime Members Who Shop at Whole Foods: You're in Luck," *Wall Street Journal*, June 16, 2018, https://goo.gl/meRcfC.

5. Jack Neff, "Study: Consumers Get More Fickle Despite Billions Spent on Loyalty," *Ad Age*, February 14, 2017, https://goo.gl/xGcEmJ.

6. Laura Berman, "Macy's Reports 11th Consecutive Same-Store Sales Decline," *TheStreet*, November 11, 2017, https://goo.gl/A8K8eL.

7. "Loyalty," Trader Joe's, October 14, 2017, https://goo.gl/gYVRfJ.

8. J. P. Mangalindan, "Comcast CEO: 'I Was Embarrassed' by Customer Service Debacle," *Fortune*, November 13, 2014, https://goo.gl/pPQABz; Stephanie Mlot, "Comcast Is America's Most Hated Company," *PC*, January 12, 2017, https://goo.gl/G68gdC

9. Khadeeja Safdar and Laura Stevens, "Banned from Amazon: The Shoppers Who Make Too Many Returns," *Wall Street Journal*, May 22, 2018, https://goo.gl/EYxErz.

10. Eric Jordan, "How Long Is a Lifetime Warranty for Luggage, Really?," *Condé Nast Traveler*, June 26, 2015, https://goo.gl/tCYHGf.

11. Chavie Lieber, "How Amazon Prime Took Over Online Shopping," *Racked*, July 16, 2018, https://goo.gl/Bgha6V.

12. Jonathan Vanian, "Amazon Has Over 100 Million Prime Members," *Fortune*, April 19, 2018, https://goo.gl/uQtZDC.

13. Khadeeja Safdar, "Target Undercuts Amazon with Free Two-Day Shipping," *Wall Street Journal*, October 23, 2018, https://goo.gl/FCL1Nx.

14. Michael R. Levin, "Amazon Prime Members Stay Membérs," *Huffpost*, June 7, 2016 (updated December 6, 2017), https://goo.gl/eiDBvG.

15. Tanya Powley, "European Airlines Face More Cuts and Consolidation," *Financial Times*, August 10, 2017, https://goo.gl/RpD9Xe.

CHAPTER 4   Customer-Focus Strategy 2: Personalization Is Not a Luxury

1. "Starbucks Same-Store Sales," *eMarketer Retail*, https://goo.gl/DF3Zin. Accessed February 15, 2019.

2. Liza Lin and Laura Stevens, "Why Amazon Isn't Ready for Prime Time in China," *Wall Street Journal*, August 27, 2017, https://goo.gl/DKnQHk.

3. Kelsey Lawrence, "Why Won't Millennials Join Country Clubs?" *CityLab*, July 2, 2018, https://goo.gl/eqxaGm.

4. James Cox, "Burberry Burned $36.5M of Unsold Clothes Last Year," *New York Post*, July 19, 2018, https://goo.gl/rL77UC.

5. Pamela N. Danziger, "Luxury Brands Are in Danger of Losing American Millennials: How to Get Them Back," *Forbes*, September 11, 2017, https://goo.gl/tRSc5V.

6. David Fickling, "Size Isn't Everything, Big Auto," *Bloomberg*, August 1, 2017, https://goo.gl/vZqnFG.

7. Alex Mayyasi and Priceonomics, "How Subaru Came to Be Seen as Cars for Lesbians," *Atlantic*, June 22, 2016, https://goo.gl/U8sfP4.

8. Sean McLain, "Subaru Is Betting Big on Staying Small," *Wall Street Journal*, May 21, 2017, https://goo.gl/6RLT6K.

9. Stuart Heaver, "The Rise and Fall of the Hong Kong Tailoring Industry," *Post Magazine*, August 19, 2016 (updated August 22, 2016), https://goo.gl/HjzjEM.

CHAPTER 5   Customer-Focus Strategy 3: Customers Won't Wait

1. Alan Wolf, "With Impatient Millennials, Website Delays Are Deadly," *Twice*, October 14, 2016, https://goo.gl/Poab6q.

2. Leon Poultney, "Hey Tesla, How Hard Can It Be to Actually Make a Car?," *Wired*, April 22, 2018, https://goo.gl/m3W9vF.

3. Joan Schneider and Julie Hall, "Why Most Product Launches Fail," *Harvard Business Review*, April 2011, https://goo.gl/3HKvUY.

4. Deborah Weinswig, "Retailers Should Think Like Zara: What We Learned at the August Magic Trade Show," *Forbes*, August 28, 2017, https://goo.gl/2ejMsd.

5. Todd Haselton, "Report Shows Why Apple Should Have Launched iPhone X Sooner," *CNBC*, December 5, 2017, https://goo.gl/DjbDGf.

6. Mike Colias, "GM to Idle Detroit Car Factory Amid Slow Demand," *Wall Street Journal*, October 12, 2017, https://goo.gl/16TDns.

7. Christopher Muther, "Instant Gratification Is Making Us Perpetually Impatient," *Boston Globe*, February 2, 2013, https://goo.gl/qbYhXC.

CHAPTER 6   Customer-Focus Strategy 4: Good Enough Is No Longer Good Enough

1. Michael Bartiromo, "Chick-fil-A to Become Nation's Third-Largest Fast Food Restaurant by 2020, Analysts Say," Fox News, April 3, 2018, https://goo.gl/6E6gK1.

2. "Where Our Food Comes From," Chick-fil-A, https://goo.gl/V6xoNJ.

3. Kate Samuelson, "A Brief History of Samsung's Troubled Galaxy Note 7 Smartphone," *Time*, October 11, 2016, https://goo.gl/UvwZvL.

4. Aaron Pressman, "Samsung Smartphone Sales Plummeted Worldwide Due to Galaxy Note 7, *Fortune*, January 31, 2017, https://goo.gl/qrDt6W.

5. Catherine Rampell, "A 'Big Three' Failure and U.S. Auto Making," *New York Times*, November 19, 2008, https://goo.gl/rSG33a.

6. "Apple CEO Explains Why Apple's Products Are So Expensive (Sort Of)," *Huffpost*, February 12, 2013, https://goo.gl/QqJoP4.

7. Rune Jacobsen et al., "How Discounters Are Remaking the Grocery Industry," BCG, April 21, 2017, https://goo.gl/7b9jvn.

8. "Our Awards and Achievements", Qatar Airways, https://goo.gl/LrS6CV.

9. "2016/17 Annual Report Shows Airline's Annual Revenue Has Increased by 10.4 Per Cent," Qatar Airways, June 11, 2017, https://goo.gl/UzjZFB.

10. "Our Awards and Achievements," Qatar Airways, https://goo.gl/LrS6CV.

11. "20th Death from Faulty Takata Air Bags Reported by Honda," CBS News, December 20, 2017, https://goo.gl/k7tQbj.

CHAPTER 7   Customer-Focus Strategy 5: Disregard Strategies 1 through 4

1. Joanna Stern, "Jeff Bezos: A Down-to-Earth CEO Reaching for the Stars," ABC News, September 25, 2013, https://goo.gl/Mo2NEj.

2. Grace Donnelly, "Dairy Farmers Experiencing an Organic Milk Surplus as Sales of Almond, Soy Milk Rise," *Fortune*, January 2, 2018, https://goo.gl/HsE7aw.

3. Rupali Arora, "China's Top 100 Companies," *Fortune*, August 28, 2007, https://goo.gl/nAqssp; "China Top 500 Rankings in 2018" [in Chinese], *Fortune China*, July 10, 2018, https://goo.gl/UACiqB.

4. Bill Fischer, Umberto Lago, and Fang Liu, *Reinventing Giants: How Chinese Global Competitor Haier Has Changed the Way Big Companies Transform* (San Francisco: Jossey-Bass, 2013).

5. Bill Fischer, Umberto Lago, and Fang Liu, "The Haier Road to Growth," *Strategy + Business*, April 27, 2015, https://goo.gl/g5Srkh.

6. Suparna Dutt D'Cunha, "PM Modi Calls the World to 'Make in India,' but the Initiative Fails to Take Off," *Forbes*, July 24, 2017, https://goo.gl/WS53cG.

7. "World's Most Valuable Brands," *Forbes*, https://goo.gl/vnLbQZ.

CONCLUSION: Choosing and Implementing the Strategies

1. Stephen Adams, "Millions Taking Statins 'Needlessly'," *Telegraph*, January 19, 2011, https://goo.gl/zqgRD6.

2. "Which Car Brands Have the Most (and Least) Loyal Owners?," CarMax, July 12, 2018, https://goo.gl/p9mZ63.

3. Lisa Fu, "New Cars Are Unaffordable for Most Americans," *Fortune*, June 28, 2017, https://goo.gl/zVYNv3.

4. Amazon Jobs, https://goo.gl/1wtEHi. Accessed February 15, 2019.

5. "Customer Service," Southwest, https://goo.gl/HsYfJS. Accessed February 15, 2019.

6. Jay Yarow, "Apple's Retail Secrets Spilled: Don't Correct the Customers, Abide by the A.P.P.L.E. Code," *Business Insider*, June 15, 2011, https://goo.gl/ybhyri.

7. Julie Weber, "How Southwest Airlines Hires Such Dedicated People," *Harvard Business Review*, December 2, 2015, https://goo.gl/RpSTJc.

8. Matt Clinch, "How Apple Prompted This Country's Downgrade," CNBC, October 13, 2014, https://goo.gl/vfnG1u; Jason Karaian, "Finland's Sickly Economy Is Shrinking Again," *Quartz*, August 15, 2017, https://goo.gl/KXrMUZ.

ACKNOWLEDGMENTS

THE CONCEPTS IN THIS book were developed for my clients. They trusted me with their resources and allowed me to experiment and develop the ideas that are shared in the book. I want to acknowledge my profound respect for my clients and their teams.

Libby Koponen was the developmental editor and helped with structuring the content. She excels at translating complex concepts into easy-to-understand prose. Her critique of each chapter was enormously valuable, as she was able to structure the chapters to make the book easy to follow. Additionally, I would like to acknowledge the contributions of Alan Farnham and Alyson Harrold. They were initially involved in writing and structuring the book. Alan is a great writer, with the gift of articulation, and Alyson is a genius in marketing. I can't thank them enough for their contribution.

Niharika Ramdev, my partner, patiently reviewed all the chapters and critiqued some of the concepts proposed in the book. Her perspectives made the book and concepts practical. I am grateful to Frank Lonegro, CFO of CSX Transportation, for thorough review of the manuscript and valuable feedback. Also, thanks to Charles Wijayawardhana, whose valuable insights from his global transportation industry experience at FedEx and CSX made this book an even richer one. Special thanks to Ramesh Taskar for patiently reviewing the chapters and identifying improvement areas.

I want to thank Neal Maillet and Jeevan Sivasubramaniam, editors at Berrett-Koehler, for their thoughtful critique throughout the development of the book. Without their active coaching and collaboration, this book would never have happened.

Finally, I would like to thank Michael Snell, my agent. His continued confidence in me has been a great source of comfort.

INDEX

ABOUT THE AUTHOR

Suman Sarkar is a partner with Three S Consulting. His mission is to help clients deliver on customer needs through operations.

With more than twenty years of international consulting experience, Suman has helped companies achieve success through innovative approaches.

He has worked with leading companies in multiple areas, including financial services; the wireless, pharmaceutical, technology, consumer goods, retail, and outsourcing industries; and government agencies.

Before launching his consulting practice, Suman was a management consultant at A. T. Kearney and worked at Procter & Gamble.

Suman holds a bachelor's degree in mechanical engineering from the Indian Institute of Technology Kharagpur, India, and a master's degree in industrial engineering from the National Institute of Industrial Engineering, Mumbai, India, graduating at the top of his class at both schools. Suman also has an MBA in strategy and finance from UCLA.

He is the author of one of the top-selling supply chain books on Amazon, *The Supply Chain Revolution*, and has authored several articles in leading publications about the importance of supply chain and operations.

❈ Berrett–Koehler
BK̄ Publishers

Berrett-Koehler is an independent publisher dedicated to an ambitious mission: *Connecting people and ideas to create a world that works for all.*

Our publications span many formats, including print, digital, audio, and video. We also offer online resources, training, and gatherings. And we will continue expanding our products and services to advance our mission.

We believe that the solutions to the world's problems will come from all of us, working at all levels: in our society, in our organizations, and in our own lives. Our publications and resources offer pathways to creating a more just, equitable, and sustainable society. They help people make their organizations more humane, democratic, diverse, and effective (and we don't think there's any contradiction there). And they guide people in creating positive change in their own lives and aligning their personal practices with their aspirations for a better world.

And we strive to practice what we preach through what we call "The BK Way." At the core of this approach is *stewardship,* a deep sense of responsibility to administer the company for the benefit of all of our stakeholder groups, including authors, customers, employees, investors, service providers, sales partners, and the communities and environment around us. Everything we do is built around stewardship and our other core values of *quality, partnership, inclusion,* and *sustainability.*

This is why Berrett-Koehler is the first book publishing company to be both a B Corporation (a rigorous certification) and a benefit corporation (a for-profit legal status), which together require us to adhere to the highest standards for corporate, social, and environmental performance. And it is why we have instituted many pioneering practices (which you can learn about at www.bkconnection.com), including the Berrett-Koehler Constitution, the Bill of Rights and Responsibilities for BK Authors, and our unique Author Days.

We are grateful to our readers, authors, and other friends who are supporting our mission. We ask you to share with us examples of how BK publications and resources are making a difference in your lives, organizations, and communities at www.bkconnection.com/impact.

Dear reader,

Thank you for picking up this book and welcome to the worldwide BK community! You're joining a special group of people who have come together to create positive change in their lives, organizations, and communities.

What's BK all about?

Our mission is to connect people and ideas to create a world that works for all.

Why? Our communities, organizations, and lives get bogged down by old paradigms of self-interest, exclusion, hierarchy, and privilege. But we believe that can change. That's why we seek the leading experts on these challenges—and share their actionable ideas with you.

A welcome gift

To help you get started, we'd like to offer you a **free copy** of one of our bestselling ebooks:

www.bkconnection.com/welcome

When you claim your **free ebook**, you'll also be subscribed to our blog.

Our freshest insights

Access the best new tools and ideas for leaders at all levels on our blog at ideas.bkconnection.com.

Sincerely,

Your friends at Berrett-Koehler